PRISONS

Inside the
New America

PRISONS

Inside the New America

From Vernooykill Creek to Abu Ghraib

SECOND EDITION

David Matlin

North Atlantic Books
Berkeley, California

Portions of this book appeared as *Vernooykill Creek: The Crisis of Prisons in America* (San Diego State University Press, 1997)

Published by	Cover and text design by Brad Greene
North Atlantic Books	Printed in the United States of America
P.O. Box 12327	Distributed to the book trade
Berkeley, California 94712	by Publishers Group West

Prisons: Inside the New America is sponsored by the Society for the Study of Native Arts and Sciences, a nonprofit educational corporation whose goals are to develop an educational and crosscultural perspective linking various scientific, social, and artistic fields; to nurture a holistic view of arts, sciences, humanities, and healing; and to publish and distribute literature on the relationship of mind, body, and nature.

North Atlantic Books' publications are available through most bookstores. For further information, call 800-337-2665 or visit our website at www.northatlanticbooks.com.

Substantial discounts on bulk quantities are available to corporations, professional associations, and other organizations. For details and discount information, contact our special sales department.

Library of Congress Cataloging-in-Publication Data

Matlin, David.
  Prisons : inside the new America : from Vernooykill Creek to Abu Ghraib / by David Matlin ; foreword by Ishmael Reed. Afterword by David Matlin.
    p. cm.
  Updated ed. of: Vernooykill Creek. 1997.
  Summary: "David Matlin's account of his experiences teaching in American prisons exposes the corruption of the prison business and the inhumanity of our system of punishment in the United States"—Provided by publisher.
  Includes bibliographical references.
  ISBN 1-55643-549-5 (pbk.)
  1. Prisons—United States. 2. Prisoners—Education—United States. I. Matlin, David. Vernooykill Creek. II. Title.
  HV9471.M37 2004
  365'.973—dc22
                                                        2004024463
              1 2 3 4 5 6 7 8 9 MALLOY 09 08 07 06 05

For my son, Clay,
and to the memory of my mother
Lola Kenyon Matlin

Contents

Acknowledgments

To the men I worked with in those prisons who changed
my life.

Other grateful acknowledgment is made to Kristin Prevallet
and Alan Gilbert for publishing excerpts in *apex of the M*.

I would also like to thank George Economou for the invitation
to the University of Oklahoma where I discovered essential
materials for this book.

To my friends Charles Stein and Don Byrd
for their care and suggestions.

And, most importantly, to Gail.

Foreword

WITH A GRANT from Poets and Writers, and, before that, funding from the federal government (a program gutted by the Clinton administration)—David Matlin taught writing to prisoners in New York State.

He writes "... the men I worked with in those man-made hells—their families and their communities before the larger tragedy of what I then considered and still consider to be the single and most reductive symptom of a People and Nation infected with a savagery which has been commercialized, crafted, and transposed into an expertise which has now disassembled our humanity. ..."

This ringing indictment, which appears in the introduction, is followed by a cataloguing of the cruel policies that characterize our correction system's approach to punishing those in our society who run afoul of the law. In this system, prisoners are commodities that fuel a growing corrections industry. It advertises its services in the same way that a car dealership might advertise automobiles. So powerful is this industry that it reduced the steroids-pumped Gov. Schwarzenegger to a girlie man. Recent investigations by the state of California have revealed mistreatment of prisoners by guards in both the adult and juvenile divisions, yet, the corrections union boasted, after contract negotiations, that they gave the Governor one dollar and received one dollar and fifty cents in exchange. The former Governor Gray Davis received such large campaign donations from the union that they owned him.

Politicians and the media boost this industry. Politicians win elections by playing to the fears of a white population about black crime. The news media, led by the *New York Times*, do their part to raise their readership ratings by associating black males with pathology. Entertainment shows like David Simon's *Homicide, The Corner,* and *The Wire*, and a number of Hollywood movies, have had the same effect. The result is what the *Wall Street Journal* described as a situation in which those who have the least to fear from crime are driving the issue.

As a result, black males are placed in what Matlin calls "man-made hells"; white prisoners have difficulty surviving in such hells. A prisoner with a Master's Degree is quoted by Matlin as observing that those members of society least prepared for the pain and isolation of prison are "... predominately white and middle class."

Not surprisingly, suicide among white inmates are disproportionately higher than for either black or Hispanic inmates.

Jail, on the other hand, has always been blacks' home away from home, from the time they arrived on these shores. In the old days, as now, they were often jailed without having committed any crime. Confederate General Robert E. Lee advises in a letter to a slave broker to hold his slaves in a jail until they can be sold. After Emancipation, black men were ensnared by the convict labor system, the theme of Charles Chesnutt's 1905 novel, *The Colonel's Dream.*

To continue the conditions of slavery, the post-Reconstruction criminal justice system provided businessmen with cheap labor by arresting blacks on trumped-up charges. In Chesnutt's novel, even the town's lovable Uncle is arrested and has to be "bought" out of this condition by the novel's hero, a liberal ex-Confederate officer. This practice continues to this day, where the corrections industry justifies the building of more jails by herding blacks into prisons on the basis of crimes that, if they were white, would be considered pranks, in the words of Sheriff Michael Hennessy of San Francisco County.

Perhaps this is why there is such racial disparity in arrest and incarceration rates. The majority of those arrested in both cities and the rural areas are white; while those imprisoned are disproportionately black and Hispanic. Police, district attorneys, and judges know that their white brothers and sisters can't take it, and spare them the harsh punishment they mete out to black, brown, and red people. The November 2004 Sentencing Project's report described in the *New York Times*, corroborated that blacks receive harsher sentences than whites.

One of many public and media myths holds that white people do powder cocaine while blacks prefer crack. There's evidence that whites do crack too, but few have received the tough sentences meted out to blacks convicted of violating the drug laws. A May, 1995 article in the *Los Angeles Times* described this situation: "Despite evidence that large numbers of whites use and sell crack cocaine, federal law enforcement in Southern California has waged its war against crack almost exclusively in minority neighborhoods, exposing black and Latino offenders to the toughest drug penalties in the nation. Not a single white, records show, has been convicted of a crack cocaine offense in federal courts serving Los Angeles and six Southern California counties since Congress enacted stiff mandatory sentences for crack dealers in 1986."

DNA science has recently exposed the astounding numbers of black men jailed for crimes they didn't commit. One suspects that if it were not for police and prosecutorial misconduct, the rates of imprisonment among blacks would be cut in half, but blacks and Matlin have to convince an indifferent inattentive public that racism in the criminal justice system exists. Good numbers of the public still believe Saddam Hussein had something to do with 9/11. A view of a frightened, ignorant white public, both on the right and left. When discussing black men, *The Nation*, Pacifica, and NPR radio all often sound like Fox News, except that Fox has more black men among its personnel. Indeed, David Matlin exposes ex-New York Governor Mario Cuomo and President Bill Clinton as having benefited from get tough anti-crime rhetoric. These politicians are considered moderate or liberal by the mass media.

Matlin points to Mario Cuomo as being responsible for the appearance of more new prison space than all previous governors combined in New York State's history. It was President Clinton's Crime Bill that destroyed the monies designated on a nation-wide basis for all prison education. This might be the reason that the 3,000 felons in Oakland, who have made it into a "frightening city," are "illiterate" and "dangerous" in the words of David Hilliard, of the Black Panther Party. The suburbs may wreak "vengeance" from such get-tough measures, but these prisoners don't return to their neighborhoods; they return to mine.

Matlin also writes about the AIDs crisis among the prison population. In a Sept. 7, 2004 op-ed column the *Times'* editorial writer, Brent Staples, cited a study by *The Prison Journal* that put the percentage of those prisoners having sex with other men in California at 40 percent.

By deliberately placing prisoners who defy the system into cells with rapists, guards use rape as punishment. These infected prisoners are released to the general population, where they pass the virus on to African-American women. You don't have to be a conspiracy crank to conclude that these and other insidious policies are contributing to the genocide of African-Americans.

Matlin's book is engaging. He not only presents facts and statistics about the national shame that the prison system has become, but provides eye witness testimonies and anecdotes. If he were addressing an enlightened population, this book would energize prison reform the way Ralph Nader went up against the automobile industry, and Jessica Mitford galvanized a national inquiry into the scams of funeral business. It would rank with Upton Sinclair's expose of the meat packing industry.

When a world-wide furor erupted after the abuses at Abu Ghraib, where members of a generation that grew up on electronic games gave vent to their sadistic impulses by humiliating prisoners of war, I, along with many African-Americans, wondered how long it would take for the public to become outraged by the Abu Ghraibs that exist in this country. Most telling in this scandal was that one of those involved in these abominable acts was a former American prison guard.

—Ishmael Reed
February, 2005
Oakland, California

Introduction

IN THE SUMMER OF 1998 I received a grant from Poets & Writers to go back into New York State's prisons. It had been three years since Clinton's Crime Bill of 1995 had destroyed not only the Program I had worked in for so many years, but similar fully accredited Higher Education Prison Programs across the nation. I wrote this book as a personal response not only to Clinton's cynical and base legislation, but as part of a private vow to the men I worked with in those man-made hells, their families, their communities before the larger tragedy of what I then considered and still consider to be the single and most reductive symptom of a People and Nation infected with a savagery which has been commercialized, crafted, and transposed into an expertise which has now disassembled our humanity, our shared compassions, the bonds of common mercy which formed the hoped for roots of a possible Democracy envisioned by the authors of the Constitution and Declaration of Independence.

Many of New York State's prisons are situated in some of the most beautiful countryside in North America. One of my Poets & Writers destinations took me to Western New York and the gorge of the Genesee River in Letchworth State Park. I'm a westerner who spent almost thirty years in New York, both its wonderful City and its Catskill Mountains. But I grew up with the Sierras, the Grand Canyon, the huge sweep of deserts where you can still find the bones of ancient chee- tah and elephant lying in remote canyons. I was not prepared for what I saw hidden by the gently sloped meadows of this ancient Seneca world. The cliffs of the Genesee gorge fall a sheer thousand feet into swamp, sand bar, and a waiting river that has been eating this plateau since the final recession of the last glaciers. When I was there in July its two water falls were raging. It seemed to me as I stood at their edge that they could barely hold the deliverance of run off swelling with rainbow, mist, and the demonic roar of water that must have filled the minds and souls of ancestor Paleolithic artist-hunters who knew the melt with an intimacy which may still yet haunt the secret core of dreams beyond any of our knowing. The reach of sky and time has a scale that strikes you with a first intense immobility before the folds of earth and the folds of the invisible that have welled up into all the life gathered and gone here.

One of my heroes also lived out the last years of her life next to these cliffs. Mary Jameson the white girl made captive at fourteen and never returned, became a Seneca woman holding one of the great and mostly hidden stories about women and about America. Attica lies just over the immediate horizon and I had to be at its gates early the next morning. I don't like maximum security prisons. They scare me at levels I still can't quite articulate even to this day, though I spent a good part of my working years inside these supposed "Justice Spaces." We have not yet made any settlements on the Moon, or Mars, but the one space that we have claimed as a new empire is prison and before I go into these "spaces" I try best as I can to get my breath. There's much less preparation for the man-infected malevolences of a cyclops like Attica. You can feel it sucking at everything around it. It reminds me of those slow motion films the Atomic Energy Commission made of atomic fireballs as they breathed and ruptured and grew for only those terrible seconds, but it was enough and you knew as a little kid, more than you could ever want. I spent a whole day with people in that "warehouse." I've been in mean ones, but none of them compare to this and when the end of that day came I was late, couldn't get past the gates, and when I did Gail was standing outside in a near panic. Two weeks later there was a "minor" riot. You could feel it stretching the walls and what had gone before it too in 1970 when this warehouse became the largest site of Americans killing Americans since the Civil War.

I've thought about this "Introduction" and what it means to me as Whitman's "Person"; the individual citizen trying to examine, trying to be aware knowing how imperiled Democracy always is. Since 1995 too, I've moved back clear across America again to my native California to teach in an MFA Creative Writing Program at San Diego State University. This border region contains new immigrations from not only all over the Pacific Rim, but much of Latin American, and part of Africa. The Border "Wall" extends literally into the Pacific and for detailed miles past Tijuana and on into the dangerous remote deserts where people die by the hundreds, nearly mummifying within hours of their deaths. Heavily armed "Immigration" officers patrol this barrier twenty-four hours a day. A grim, "safe" post 9/11 America lies beyond but this "patrol zone" that looks like the exterior of a prison has an exacting finality to it and I can hear the marketing frequencies bloating with various products designed for "The Industry"; "utilization review teams"; "the most advanced watchtour systems";

"urine and semen 1 test per minute systems"; "slammer stools"; "point-to-point floor-plan graphics"; "infectious liquid spill control powders"; "Rhino Buckets"; "multichanneled, simultaneous recorder and playback digital voice loggers"; "automated head counts" designer chemicals featuring "Deep Freeze," "Clear Out," "Punch M5G," the most advanced "Corrections Specific Area Treatment" weapons: the perfections of the American Prison turned inside out on the American population with the following *watchterms* of the Industry itself:

Simplicity

Flexibility

Capacity

to indicate at once how fragile and menacing we have become from "Vernooykill Creek" to "Abu Ghraib" over the last three or four generations as the company of these new vocabularies with their invocations of closure and reprisal hover over us now as never before.

The Border is also the confluence of the largest migration perhaps in human history, certainly one of the most ancient beginning with the Beringian surges south, and now in what still truly to be named age we're living through, a surge back toward the north, along with the largest amassment of police agencies ever devised to check, monitor, and harass such human desperation. In the neighborhoods adjacent to my own, there are at least thirty-seven languages spoken. California also has the largest and most dangerous Prison Industry in the world, an Industry that has drained its great civic and educational potential whose six billion dollars a year cost is smothering the living dreams of this and other states that have and are allowing prisons to inexorably transform each of our communities no matter what their identity into a carefully organized disintegration beyond appearance or comprehension. There is no discoverable gauge for the embrace of this loss and what it means in terms of the human and humane work now gone truly guideless we once deserved to offer to each other and which now lies rotting as a supposed "democracy" "pans" (to use the vocabulary of greed of my California ancestry) frantically for such forfeiture and erased maps that once provided assurance and coherence.

In 1985 I went into New York State's maximum security prisons. I had no idea what was to come. I would spend the next ten years teaching men who were mostly Black or Latino the most basic forms of remedial reading and writing, and depending on the nature of their bids or sentences, follow them, their families and their communities all the way to a fully accredited Masters Degree granted by the State University of New York. I realized from that earliest beginning, and I still don't know quite how, that the one thing I had to leave behind if I was going to continue going through those gates, was my own will to despair, and my secret pride in it. It wasn't just that there was no room for that sense of loss, it was the fact that a continued carriage would have meant demeaning and further reducing the people I would work with for all of those years to follow. The final hold they had in the midst of catastrophic and unimaginable loss was their desire to gain an education, an education which posed for them the hardest questions about personal breakage with its price of a nullification so unbearable and paralyzing that one becomes a corpse in a corpse world smelled, tasted, swallowed every inconceivable second.

Where can we begin to think again as those "Persons" of Whitman's Vista and Creative Theme and in thinking not be overwhelmed

by the disshaping ravages everywhere we see around us and their ruth-
less totalities? At the core of that totality lies the images of our prisons,
a nothing we have manufactured and continue to manufacture, and
by that I mean *a nothing*, into our largest growth industry and which
we witness now spreading with our invasions and our promises to con-
struct an "American quality" maximum security prison in Iraq.

Why, with the background shadow of our will to deadening racism,
have we embarked on this unprecedented mining of our civil disintegration and indifference that has counterfeited our private daily lives
with what we have come to believe are acceptable violations?

I have tried to bring up at least some of these questions. When I
moved to California in August of 1997 my native state had 155,000
prisoners in its warehouses. As I write this Introduction in July of 2004
there are now 163,000 men and women imprisoned in this one state
alone. Yet this number is the tip of an iceberg; there are forty adult and
youth prisons in California with a total of 308,000 present inmates
and parolees with approximately 54,000 employees needed to oversee
and control this huge number of bodies. 31,000 of these employees
belong to the Correctional Peace Officers Union, one of the most influ-
ential single lobbies in this state able to actually dictate policy, and
with an average salary per guard of $73,000 per year, far more than
teachers in elementary, middle, and secondary schools, and more than
many assistant and associate professors in California's colleges and
universities has in addition to its mass of power, unlimited "sick leave"
for all of its members. In the face of massive budget cuts the only entity
to receive increases is the prison industry. Kings county is the largest
county in the United States where more than ten percent of the population are prisoners. Lassen County with its population of 35,000 has

10,500 prisoners. Prison has become so essential in California that any significant reduction is economically unthinkable. The recidivism rate for adult prisoners is 70 percent; a number so overwhelming in terms of its total costs to individuals, families, communities, and the nation as a whole that it seems an inaccessible "blank" but a "blank" nonetheless that guarantees constant employment and benefits for a prison industry that forces all of us to feed on crushing hypocrisy and cynicism. This is a triumph generating barrenness and dread at the secret core of our daily lives so tangled we don't any longer know how exactly its touch rots everyone of us. The pictures from Abu Ghraib, swelled with perversion and self-satisfied hate, are only hints of our domestic abyss we have already perfected and begun to export. This is not a threshold looming before us as a People, it is a threshold we passed through long ago and we have been for at least two generations perfecting it ransoms. There is a picture of Paul Wolfowitz in the spring of 2003 inspecting the refurbished jail cells of Abu Ghraib. His look of absolute certainty is encoded with the treachery and betrayal his culture has been practicing against itself at the most distant borders of ghostliness for decades. The prisoners in America and the prisoners in Abu Ghraib and Guantanamo are all ghosts who are, because of the exile we have assigned them legally and illegally, natural resources as essential now as oil or natural gas but this resource will not run dry.

Chowchilla, California, at the time of my move, was the fasting growing community in the nation with its two newest state of the art women's prisons, a "state of the art" that feeds on the latest startling numbers about women going to prison in America from 1986 to 1997. These numbers rose from 410,300 to 895,300, a 118 percent increase or more than 10 percent for each of these 11 years. The projections for the year 2027 are for over 400,000 prisoners, male and female adults and children. It seems California is far ahead of it own estimates. Perhaps there'll be five hundred or maybe even six hundred thousand people locked down with a cost of 30 billion. In D.H. Lawrence's great and disturbing "St. Mawr" there is a vision of evil, one of the most compassionately rendered I have ever seen, and because of that one of the most shattering. The waves of evil that have swept and are sweeping away mankind without our really ever knowing, without our ever really wanting or wishing such a thing to have happened. If we are living in such a time then how am I, again, as "Person" going to render an examination with enough care and precision that the reassurance, the ". . . desire for creation and productive happiness" as Lawrence calls it, in everyday life, is not cut from its roots. The fact of prison as the central core of our collapse of imagination tells us directly that we have already cut away more of those roots than we might want to count.

In that same summer of 1998 I was waiting for clearance outside of another prison in the hills surrounding Fallsburg, New York. I'd gone through a section of the southern Catskills to get to this cage. It was a world where two conflicting civilizations seemed for a little time to have at last found peace in the hollows and ice-shaved valleys of this primordial hill-country. Jews and Gentiles once met here to fish, to farm, to toil, to sometimes intermarry, and even more wondrously, to laugh. The route is through the "Hotel Country" where a traveler can still almost see the signs for Peckler's, Wadler's, Hotel Majestic, Pollak's, Evans Kiamesha, Schenck's Paramount, Rosenblatt's Glen Wild, Grossinger's. Danny Kaye, Sid Caesar, Pegleg Bates, Red Buttons, Jerry Lewis, Eddie Fisher, Professor Irwin Corey, Jack Benny,

George Burns, Gracey Allen, Jimmy Durante; the names who became "names," and those who didn't, created an imagination of laughter in these forests and a local economy based on generations of city kids who came here with new dreams and enchantments which would never have been allowed in the shtetls of their origins. These hills became a site of human and humane invention. All of it, including its local economy, have nearly vanished, but the hotels are still referred to as "Hotels"; an admittance and keepsake that tells us who come afterward how staggered and precarious the voyage has become in this time of brutal removes and abandonments.

The bird life that late afternoon was startling, cruelly unhurried. The forest, wind-swept and thick formed a closure where vultures, ravens, and hawks perched on its pine-sweltered edges. It was a perfect backdrop for the hanging gardens of flesh-shredding steel contracted for the escape-prone who had come to this terminus to endlessly scrub the walls floors ceilings, and plant flower beds under the thin wind-pumped shadows of carefully arranged razors trembling in the air as part of the directive for cleanliness issued by the local warden. These are the men or their sons who will mine the Moon and Mars, if prisons are allowed to swallow up those who are to be born into a future as "surplus."

George Washington did something similar in the mid-eighteenth century. His acts were also a speculation on millions of acres of so-called "wilderness" the original inhabitants had known and cultivated intimately for thousands of years. He sent prisoners into what may as well have been the equivalent of an asteroid, to chop down the beloved forests of the alien, and to receive the alien's tomahawk as token of that rage and the beginning of some of the most ghoulish wars ever fought. The expansion of prison as growth industry dares and promotes civil and ecological collapse. I remember an essay the poet Frank O'Hara wrote about the American artist Robert Motherwell: that one might experience the "traumatic consciousness of emergency and crisis as personal event," and assume responsibility for being alive "here and now," no matter how accidentally. I don't know if this could ever be proposed as some cozy information that will rise up to deliver any of us from the parasitic breakages we are living through. But maybe that sense of a "personal event" O'Hara so drastically imagines is the beginning of a first dislodgement from our embrace of this lethal story from Vernooykill Creek, the beautiful small stream meandering in front of the maximum security prison in Napanoch, New York, to Abu Ghraib, near the life engendering Tigris. In this too, I remember a passage from one of the eighteenth-century old Northwest Chronicles of settlement about an American "fort" constructed in the midst of a "vast emptiness" later to be called "Ohio." For a mile in every direction that island was surrounded by the broken glass of whiskey bottles. It was at once portrait and signature of a mutilation "Indians" and "Whites" had succumbed to in their then and still on-going one-sided racial holocaust. When I think of prisons in the beautiful wildernesses from New York to the terrible desert penitentiaries over the magnificent Mohave horizon, from "Bagdad" California (or in a spectacular isolated valley in Oaxaca where to my shock I saw an expensive "America Style" maximum security womens' prison as I'd ever seen) I recall this image of an "American fort" and its work of mutilation upon ourselves.

When Donald Rumsfeld describes how "sensitively" our "smart bombs" deliver their rain of death or George Bush confidently states that the vices of Abu Ghraib cannot possibly reflect "American Values" I am reminded of Arthur Rimbaud, and his "Illuminations" where this poet who seemed to see the most serene malevolences and violations, the most detached, untroubled barbarities lying in wait at the secret boundaries of our civilization wrote, "We have faith in the poisons. We know how to give our whole life everyday." Have we embraced such voluntary malevolence and its marrowless, bloodless will and done this in a way that no other people has ever done before? I don't know how complete the embrace is or can be but the following numbers tell us about a normalization of cruelty we have created through our collective vocations of "optimism" and "innocence" which has made it easier for us to trivialize these extremely dangerous facts and our place in them.

Twelve percent of young Black males between the ages of 20 and 30 are now in jail or prison. The proportion of young Black men who are incarcerated has been rising in recent years. The percentage for young White men in the same age group is 1.6 percent. The number of persons in jail or prison in the United States exceeds 2.1 million people, fully one quarter of the prisoners in the world. One in six of these prisoners is mentally ill, 3 times as many as in the nation's mental health hospitals. Prison staff and guards are untrained, unprepared, and often see such "prisoners" and their needs as a threat to security and discipline. Their suffering is ignored or mocked, and often excessive force is used to control them. Attempted suicide and self-mutilation are perceived as disciplinary problems. The mentally ill are easier targets for rape, reprisal, solitary confinement and segregated supermax units where their symptoms deepen and persist

The number of inmates serving life sentences has increased 83 percent in the past ten years, 1 out of 11 offenders, or 128,000 not as a result of more violent crimes but because of longer mandatory sentences and more restrictive parole policies. In 1992 70,00 people had life sentences. In 2000 791,000 Black men were in jail or prison in America while 603,032 were enrolled in universities or colleges. In 1980 143,000 Black men were in our jails while 463,000 were in colleges and universities. During the prison building boom of the last twenty years the number of Americans of all races and gender in our jails or prisons has quadrupled from 582,000 to over 2.1million. The United States spends 167 billion a year on law enforcement and criminal justice or as much as health care. Since 1977 expenditures for "Corrections" have increased twice as fast as spending on health care. Between 1984 and 1994 California built twenty-one prisons and one state university. Between 1985 and 2000 the Nation's spending on "Corrections" increased by 166 percent compared to a 24 percent increase in higher education. In the 1990s states with higher increases in incarceration had lower drops in crime. Increased incarceration does not equate with public safety since the majority of prisoners imprisoned in the 1980s and 1990s during the "Prison Boom" were convicted of non-violent crimes.

The juvenile justice system in the State of California is a shambles of stupidity and unutterable collapse. Youth of color number 83 percent of those wards going to adult courts. The recidivism rates for children who enter these gates is a staggering 90 percent. The cost per year to house a juvenile offender is $80,000. A sentence to a juvenile facility in California is a threat to the mental well-being and life of the child.

In terms of demographics for our Nation's inmates, more than 40 percent of the national prison population is African American and in some of our cities more than 50 percent of young Black men are under criminal justice supervision. In 1982 the total costs for jails and prisons was $9 billion per year. In 1999 this figure was $49 billion per year. From 1974 to 2002 the number of inmates in state and federal prisons increased six-fold.

The newest study on unemployment in the African American male population by Andrew Sum, director of the Center for Labor Market Studies at Northeastern University in Boston, has found that by 2002 one of every four Black men in the United States was "idle" all year long. It is also possible the number may be even higher. This 25 percent figure identifies an on-going rapacity which neither "compassionate conservatism" nor the constant haze of propaganda washing over us can make completely "invisible" no matter its ardent attempts. In addition 44 percent of Black males are constantly jobless as are 42 of every 100 Black men from the ages of 55 to 64. Does this livid wreckage either verify with what ease we are mining this new "mineral" or does it represent with what ease it waits to be "pumped" out of its ground with a viciousness so poised, so diverse, so flexible it has become impervious?

There is one more number, however. Based upon the continuation of these "trends" a Black male born in America in the year 2001 has a 1 in 3 chance of being imprisoned in his lifetime (for a Latino male the number is one in six, for the White male, the number is one in seventeen). This number calls to us at once as a deadly warning and an envenomed hieroglyph carrying the repositories of inexhaustible stupor in The Book of Wrongs we are crawling after without any suspicion about how our rites of "safety" and "values" lie outside of the recognitions which are necessary for us to understand how our daily lives have already descended into the monstrocities initiated by this sub-world and its exact absorptions of the society that so sneakily believes it has not been contaminated.

The unacknowledged disgrace, patronage, and bottomless cruelty of these sums represent first, the invasion we have already allowed into our daily lives. The invasion outward that has come with the slippery promises to build new "American Style" maximum security prisons as "gifts" which demonstrate the qualities of our "democracy" should make us tremble over how lamed and disfigured we are and that there is to this point no visible horizon. That our rulers see them as treasures enjoining one People to an Other is a measure of the repulsion which marks our vindictive, exultant embrace of a Hell that smiles back at us in these "pictures" from Iraq without even the barest self-consciousness. A Hell this sure of itself has had decades to corrode us beyond recognition. In that, how do we find even the barest comprehension for Abu Ghraib and the latest official denials of higher responsibility by the Army Inspector General, Paul T. Mikolashek, who now describes the abuses and murders of prisoners in Afghanistan and Iraq as "aberrations" initiated only by "a few soldiers" and not a "systemic failure" that in reality extends from the deepest ravages of an internal "industry" based on the need for bodies that goes unanswered and which we believe poses no consequence other than the surety of our "safety" and "well-being." The "hastily convened" hearing in which these statements were made took place before the Senate Armed Services Committee on July 22, 2004: the presiding Chairman: Senator John W. Warner of Virginia. This is the same "Senator" who in March of 2004 arranged to let the followers of Rev. Sun Myung Moon use a

Senate office building for a religious ceremony. In that "ceremony" Sun Myung Moon declared himself the "Messiah" and said his "teaching had helped Hitler and Stalin be reborn as new persons." I want to feel there is no connection to these two phenomenon; that this powerful "Senator" does not hover over the two collapses of reality. Yet what connects these incidences is a larger torrent of rupture which is at once the inflammation of the strange and its convulsive fascinations, and a closure that uproots any possible examination of an indecipherable, reckless worship of decay we cannot stop ourselves from fondling and which ridicules us now with our own tricks of helplessness and bewilderment.

In my attempt to bear witness to my own experience and to The Book of Wrongs which offers us so little rescue at this point I think of four people who helped to guide me in this Journey. First, my wife Gail, and my son, Clay, the "Courage Givers" at the center of my life.

And two eighteenth century men: Benjamin Franklin who prayed in his last days "that God grant that not only a love of liberty but a thorough knowledge of the rights of man may pervade all the nations of the earth ..."; that the whole world be "Home" for everyone. He detested the possibility of allowing the rich a "predominancy in government" and openly expressed his fear at the Constitutional Convention for a People who failing at the craft of Democracy "can only end in despotism, as other forms have done before it, when the people shall become so corrupt as to need despotic government, being incapable of any other ..."

Joseph Brant, the great Mohawk warrior and diplomat who penned a reflection before he died in 1807 on the differences between the life of the Indian and the Americans, his main example was the American penal system, the burden finally residing on the one most "dreadful contrast":

> *Liberty to a rational creature, as much exceeds property as the light*
> *of the sun does that of the most twinkling star. But you put them on*
> *a level—to the everlasting disgrace of civilization. I seriously declare*
> *I had rather die by the most severe tortures ever inflicted on this*
> *Continent, than languish in one of your prisons for a single year . . .*
> *Does then the religion of Him whom you call your Savior inspire*
> *this spirit and lead to such practices? Surely no. It is recorded of*
> *Him a bruised reed He never broke. Cease then to call yourselves*
> *Christians, lest you publish to the world your hypocrisy. Cease too,*
> *to call other nations savage, when you are tenfold more the chil-*
> *dren of cruelty than they.*

—David Matlin

San Diego, California

January, 2005

Chapter I
Route 209

IN THE SPRING OF 1993, I was asked to teach in a Master's program for a nearby college. The surface report of such a negotiation and its assignment seems almost too rigidly normal, but the "college" was in a maximum-security prison in New York State, and the "students," working toward Master's degrees in the social sciences, were some of the finest I have ever known. Sixteen men were struggling toward this accomplishment. They had all been chosen on the merits of their undergraduate standing and recommendations. Nine of those sixteen would be published in refereed journals while still in the process of composing their final qualifying theses.

They were gifted, unrelentingly curious, and warehoused in the catastrophe of a prison. The course requirements included not only many books to be read but a final essay, one of a number to be written in preparation for their degrees. They were expert in statistics, detailed observation, analysis, interpretation. Many were fine short-story writers, essayists, and musicians. One of the readings included in my course was Alexis de Tocqueville's *Democracy In America*.

Reading that essay with these men, some who have been "down" and will remain "down" for what will be the most productive years of their lives, brought this document, of the 1830s, into a nearness and demand that might otherwise have remained hidden in its tradition of an easily called-for reference, even muse, worth finally no real trouble before a present that seems irreconcilably to unravel and pervert any remnant meanings we might have wanted to attach to it. But de Tocqueville's book, in spite of the date of its composition and the land and people he found full of such potential for both shaping and unshaping themselves, exists still as a passage of profound witness. In the tradition of so many Frenchmen who came looking for a new world from the seventeenth- and eighteenth-century coeurs du bois lost forever in the ancient remoteness of North America and adopted by the Indian, to the young noble who went no farther than frontier Montreal, de Tocqueville reached for and found a humanity that may, had he stayed in the confines of Europe, never have appeared.

His odyssey began with an assignment to survey our prison system, and bring back those findings for possible implementation in France. That his journey turned into a portrait, one of ourselves we can define as fundamental, is our luck, with all the burden such reference might contain: Democracy in America. His essay on prison remains little known. In the late twentieth century, as we enter into an obscene fury of prison-building and its "New Jack" economics, de Tocqueville might want to reverse the legend of his two books, and tell the people he seemed so to love about the grotesque sub-world they are contriving and what that world and their embrace of it will do to them.

I did not know, when I set out to teach in a prison education program, how it would touch me, give me a portrait of both myself and my nation. Each prison that we design and build bankrupts and imperils us as deeply as our nuclear bombs. We have substituted one frenzy of construction for another and made the specter of our communal protections into an almost demented abyss. These constructions among us are in reality poisoned ruins that will leave us more deeply sickened than the weapons of the death of being. This apocalypse is more hidden, this trespass and mutilation less urgent. Yet our present economics put many of us in a position to believe that prison is a new treasure containing at once an easy lure of solutions and a way of life that will continue to pose no question apart from job security and the benefits of this industrialization.

My journey into this other world really begins on a bus ride between New York City and a small Hudson River Valley town I was then living in called Saugerties, New York. I had begun a conversation with a fellow passenger, having no idea about the initiations to follow. He taught art history and because of an abandoned academic contract had taken over a college class in a local prison. The experience had fascinated him, but he was moving to another state. I asked which college was responsible for the program and got the proper names and numbers. In the late summer of 1985, I rode south on route 209, or what's locally called the Ho Chi Minh Trail because of the ugly frequency of its car wrecks. I was to receive an introductory briefing as a civilian volunteer at a "correctional facility" called Napanoch. Told to look for signs I couldn't find, I stopped at a road-side cafe and asked a waitress about the "facility." She poured some coffee and with a not-too-humiliating smirk said, "The prison's about five more miles down the road."

I had not thought about the history of prison in my personal background except with the slightest infrequency. But driving down 209 helped me recall this tragedy on both my mother's and father's sides. My paternal grandfather spent two years solitary confinement in a czarist prison for his political activities before he came to America. He lost one lung there to tuberculosis, the disease among the Russian Jews of his and previous generations making all the decisions beyond any human control. He came to America with that crucial loss basically to die. Instead, he became one of the first of his tribe to farm the Mohave Desert, a rose grower, a patriarch, coming to a long life in spite of the earlier damage. My maternal great uncle, a Mexican Indian, got himself convicted of a passion killing in nineteenth-century California and spent seventeen years in San Quentin. My mother told me he'd take the hottest, most mouth-searing peppers, chew them, and laugh at his nieces, the fury of his youth now concentrated on this family of the tomato and maybe the sexual connotations of what was left of the well of vengeance that landed him an inside price he'd never get back. That sign for "Napanoch" had not showed yet, but these tinctures of what I'd thought were an almost barren memory insisted on their flood, the faces of those two men staring at me out of the haze of their ghost journeys. If their ancestral whisperings offered advice about the gates I was about to walk through, I didn't hear.

Napanoch or "Eastern Correctional Facility" looks like a wing of the Natural History Museum in New York City. The ancient hills behind it are filled with bobcat, black bear, wild turkey. Hawks and peregrine falcons fly above the prison yard and its thirty-foot walls. The Lenni Lenape built their Long Houses on the Vernooykill Creek that runs through the valley of this prison. They were among the first native peoples to suffer the confusions and bewilderments before the Dutch settlement and its appetite for the whole world those people had known for at least a hundred generations. From the prison yard you can see the background cliffs where the raptors nest and send the generations of themselves into the air, and as I've heard from many of the men I've come to know, that sight of circling, wildly magnificent birds is an almost unbearable drop of torture.

Many of these houses of captivity are objects now of historic veneration, masterworks of the men who designed them and brought them into being. One of Pittsburgh's finest historical landmarks is the Allegeny County Jail and Courthouse. The architect, Henry Hobson Richardson, designed this building. Its beauty, function, usage of materials can almost make you forget what it really is. You could go on a tour of our country with a focus on these "masterpieces," their urban and rural locations telling an understory that begins in 1790. Philadelphia is the site of the first "penitentiary." The Walnut Street Jail would be, as the Quakers saw it, a place of total isolation for the offender. Sheltered from all forms of influence, he could have a Bible and four walls for company. By the middle of the nineteenth century, however, so many men had died or completely lost their sanity that the Quaker idea, in spite of its finest deliberations, had to be replaced.

In the late twentieth century, we are re-inventing prison and giving it a new authorship. Whether or not in what centuries there are to come we will be judged on the basis of its monstrous loss and the shadowed background of the historical crime of racism that supplies the bodies is now a crossroads evoking only the barest symptoms of disorders and their eruptions of alien intent we do not even know how to begin to come to know. The entity of a prison places the supposition of our humanity into an immersion of disfigurements. To this point historically, we have as a people been, if not able to contain, then to disguise these ruptures. We are becoming, increasingly, the dependents of our disfigurements and their snare of hatred, superstition, and compulsive retributions.

The Lieutenant at Napanoch wore a white cotton shirt and polished cotton blue pants. We came before him, myself and other civilian volunteers; were fingerprinted, photographed, record-checked. He told us the rules first. Don't give out candy. Don't form a relationship of any kind with a prisoner, personal or impersonal. Don't bring gifts. There was a whole sheet full of don'ts. Along with that scripture, he suggested that in case of an emergency we run. Any hall would do, but go as fast as you could, especially if you were being chased by a client, a client with a lead pipe, for instance. If such a thing were to take place, look for the nearest phone. Wait for the dial tone, or wait for an "officer."

It was a Friday afternoon. My class assignment was to begin the following Monday at 8:30 in the morning. Later, I would come to know that upon entering a prison you never forget where you are—never. In one of the three jails I went to, I was assigned a beeper, for just the emergency that long-ago lieutenant had provisioned. I was in an introductory composition and literature course, and spilled some papers on the floor by accident. When I leaned down to pick up the mess, the beeper in my coat pocket spilled out also. The prisoners looked at the object, them and myself knowing it was an open secret, part of the pledge of distrust and hatred between the keeper and the keeped. One man, who would later go on to get two Master's degrees, said, "Don't worry, Doctor Matlin. If we really wanted you, you wouldn't even have time to press the button."

I could not have known also the questions I would come to ask myself, the turmoil and pain they would cause me. I carry the same superstitions and fears as anyone else about habitual sex offenders, ghoulish murderers, mutilators, and baby-rapers. Such predators scare me more now after ten years of prison teaching than they ever would have had I been able to carry the distance of never knowing them. One man I taught should have set the hair on the back of my head to curl every time I saw him. He had an uncommon eye to every detail of his education, and he was very smart. I never had seen, nor wanted to, the files on the "students" I was assigned to. Such curiosity would have been a violation, even a perversion of my calling in this program, where I would come to teach everything from the most basic levels of remediation to a Master's level. All the forms of such judgment and their prejudice were to be dropped. The design of the rehabilitation must be all-inclusive for every prisoner who qualified no matter the substance of his "crime." Though such a stance might be repugnant, especially in terms of a more notorious prisoner, the design of the program concentrated on overall rehabilitation for all the men who might want to participate. Ultimately, that voluntary participation resulted in an 87 percent reduction in recidivism rates for those who did choose the disciplines and rigors of their accomplishment.

The expectation and implicit demand was for a teacher such as myself to see every man as human, nothing more and nothing less. They had already been tried, their fates broken. In one instance, a newly hired fellow teacher told me he had looked at the files for the students in his course. This was an exercise beyond his rights, but any teacher could conceivably realize. If one of the men in his class was "down" for rape and sodomy, upon such discovery how would this teacher be able to deal with that private information he had absolutely no business knowing? And why would he be sniffing? Would the per-version of one man's messy violence be set aright by the perversion of another's voyeurism and the act of power this man had assumed over his "students?" The provocation of such terms and their conse-quence would come to haunt me for the whole nearly ten years of my experience and I expect will haunt me far longer.

The prisoner of my earlier reference also had a mask of impecca-ble politeness. I should have been able to detect the leak in that mask. I tell myself now I should have had more acute antennae, antennae which later did develop but not in time for this one instance. He called me after his release, asking for a recommendation—one I should never have given. I later found out he was a vicious sex offender. If I and perhaps others could have made such potentially traumatic misread-ings, how were we to carry that information and carry it still having actually come into contact with this kind of sickness and its intended invisibilities? Many of the prisoners told me about their crimes. I was introduced to their children, wives, mothers and fathers. Some were innocent and finally able to prove that innocence; some knew they deserved and even needed to be imprisoned.

The stakes were very high. For many men, this was their last chance. Children, wives, and families shadowed almost every grade. The catastrophe of loss, years of confinement, served in most instances to create an intrinsic maturity, men standing inside what was left of themselves, though their outward lives might appear totally broken. My working days for over nine years would be spent mostly with men who were Black or Latino. The minority were Italian, Irish, Jewish, and Chinese. Some South Americans who couldn't speak a word of English in the beginning were highly educated Colombians. There were the Polish, too, and American Indians, Czechs, Texans, Cajuns, and crooked cops. One prisoner, in for seven years on a drug conviction, began in a remedial reading and writing course. He wanted to prove to his wife and young daughter, who had moved to Canada, that he was worthy still of being a father and husband even though he would be warehoused seven years, as he was to say later, in a "hell" he could have never imagined being possible. In that time, from a modest beginning, indeed, he went on to gain his community-college and Bachelor's degrees with distinction and founded clinics for children who may also be prime candidates for prison, working in conjunction with their families, schools, and if possible the surrounding communities to stop the accumulation of incidents that will lead finally to the deadened years of a "bid." While doing his time, he learned that his daughter was offered a scholarship at a private school, where one night a fire broke out. This man's child was the only one to die. A large part of his dedication was based on that daughter and his promise to her.

Every prisoner is a human being, and "time," short or long, is a wounding, scarring abyss. The contract killer and saddest junkie stand outside the sufficiency of any of our wished-for logics. The labyrinths of nullification where we would prefer them to stay in turn are robbing us of our own lives. The rescue we believe prison to hold serves our indifference toward one another. Any people's habitual ingratiation of indifference, Václav Havel, in *Living in Truth,* so unapologetically reminds us, creates a "paradox" by which indifference becomes an "active social force."[1]

At almost any point in our history, from the idea of the Walnut Street Jail in 1790 to the modern penal colony of Canon, Colorado, with its eight operating state prisons, we have lived as a people from one "crime wave" to another. Never, however, have we been more vulnerable to the manipulation of our fears, and never, in turn, have we been more vulnerable to how these manipulations will censor all but the most hallucinatory obsessions of our domestic policy. We are on the threshold of being transformed, far more completely than any previous threat could have proposed, from one people into another. This transformation and its hold upon us contain the potential to mutilate the efficacy and reality of the simplest truths that make our daily life and its actual knowledge possible. They jeopardize our ability to tell these truths to one another, to bear witness to what our daily life is, and to give ourselves the precise articulation and coherence this witness must have. We hold both the life-enriching imaginations of our civility and the lethal secrets of its disintegration as even now that disintegration moves toward ransoms which most systematically fit the directives of our unbelief and the bribery of its fatigue. That fatigue is the one born of the experiment of self de Tocqueville most feared for us as a people, that our individualities might become the means by which we would starve and suffocate our body politic at its core and humiliate our civic mores to a point where factional self-interest can no longer resolve the conflict between the private and public spheres. The evaporation of a civic vision, de Tocqueville and Madison warned, the one each of us slowly surrenders, can only lead to an emerging tolerance of dictatorship.

The manipulation of our fear of crime is creating a diversification of loss by which the hemorrhage of our ethics becomes an essential building block for a new economic infrastructure. The companies that helped produce the weapons of mass death—GDE Systems, Alliant

Techsystems, Westinghouse, Minnesota Mining & Manufacturing—
are inventing "crime-fighting" technologies for a twenty-first century
that offer a deluge of riches. The construction of new prisons now
attracts such financial monoliths as Prudential Insurance, Smith Bar-
ney Shearson, Inc., Merrill Lynch & Co., and Goldman Sachs. This
new commerce is capable of underwriting the cost of prison construction through private, tax-exempt bonds. The necessity of voter approval
and the questions posed by the process of "democracy" and its Constitution are at most an inconvenience. The increased funding for
prison maintenance, management, and building is shaping what some
have referred to as the "theme stocks of the 90s."   *Damn!*

Rural communities suffering the continued deterioration of agricultural and small-business economies are literally clawing for a prison,
hoping such an "entity" will be the savior of their fates. Such contrac-
tors as Wackenhut Corrections Corporation, underwritten by Prudential Securities, has a guarantee from the State of Florida that its prisons
"...will never be less than ninety percent filled."[2] A simple but indis-   *MURTIN!*
pensable question would be, "What does such a guarantee mean?"
And will such a guarantee shame us quietly into beginning a journey
where we will make our democracy and its spirit into a lifeless shell?
The Wackenhut Corporation, as an example, located in Coral Gables,
Florida, contracts its security services to U.S. Army ammunition plants,
Department of Energy facilities such as Rocky Flats, and at least a dozen
U.S. Department of State Embassy and Mission sites in foreign countries. It is one of the largest security firms in the world. The most
dynamic margin for profit, however, focuses on its Corrections Corporation, which manages twelve prisons and detention centers in five
states and in Australia. Experts in "privatization" believe the manage-

ment of prisons is a business worth ten billion dollars a year. Wackenhut's executive vice president, Frederick F. Thornburg, calls this market and its trends "... a moving freight train ... We believe and anticipate
that the entire area of privatization of correctional and detention facilities is going to be pretty dynamic and phenomenal ... I think the
explosion is occurring. Those dynamics, if the climate remains the
same, will continue for a long time."[3]

Mr. Thornburg's image of "... a moving freight train ..." leaves me
almost breathless in its reference. Does it matter whether such wording is conscious or unconscious? I think it does matter. It forces me
to remember the piles of gold and silver fillings, human hair and skin
stockpiled for an "industry" in another world where freight trains were
also used to bring those goods to their final destination. Such images
and their unquestioned usage by major players like Mr. Thornburg
should alert us to how close we are to an enormous surrender.

Are we going to dispose of our racist traditions or admit finally it
is something we cannot and, more crucially, are incapable of doing? Are
those traditions so intertwined with a nexus of historical profit, no
matter its source, which if questioned too closely would engender an
action of illumination that in itself threatens the totality of façades
and the surety they offer, the surety that these traditions and their
sanctions are normal? As consumers in the time of this after-admis-
sion, will we be able more accurately to evaluate prison as a part of
our shopping disciplines, the fate of our then-more-truly disposable
"others" as sources of new investment once we've rid ourselves of the
Gettysburg Address and the eighteenth-century ideals that shadow it,
and which now impose nothing more than a remnant effigy on this segment of our marketplace, where as Mr. Thornburg so accurately points

out, "... an explosion is occuring..."? Has integration and the disavowal of racism, as emblems of a body politic that tell us we must survive our maiming hypocrisies, so fatigued us that we've had enough, had enough of the work, after at most thirty years, at dislodging ourselves from the sickening racial codes that have never not haunted us? Are we this tired? And in our purchase of such fatigue, what are we about to embrace? If this "New Jack" economics, based on every new/ flesh man or woman who comes to stay in the perversions locked in the name itself, describes our "habits of the heart," then the people de Tocqueville so loved and feared for are becoming more and more incapable of at once sustaining and inventing the national "character" that calls to heart our capacity for freedom.

There are three major issues. Crime is first. Along with its profound importance, there are the mixtures of sensationalism, distortion, and fundamental political manipulation of our fear. This triumvirate produces profit at the expense of both the victims of crime and those segments of our population now undergoing a historical and shattering deterioration. The second is firearms and the National Rifle Association's so-called constitutional position in terms of this "right," and, its dissimulating use of statistics. The NRA insists that the increased incarceration rates of the 1980s created a dramatic decrease in crime rates and concludes through this that massive incarceration is justified. An examination of the same numbers by Marc Mauer of the Sentencing Project in Washington, D.C., provides a startling and much more complex view:

> The NRA claims, for example, that the 150 percent increase in incarceration from 1980 to 1991 led to a 24 percent drop in "serious victimization." Upon closer examination, however, the NRA definition

of "serious victimization" includes violent crimes, but also the non-violent crime of burglary ... While burglary rates did decline during the 1980's their inclusion with violent crimes distorts actual trends. Had the NRA included the Index Crime offense of auto theft rather than burglary in its calculations, the results would have been very different, since auto theft victimization increased by 33 percent during this period. Looking only at violent crime, we find that the more than doubling of the prison population paralleled a 4 percent decline in violent crime during this period.[4]

Mr. Mauer concludes that

The "relationship" claimed by the NRA also turns out to be one that is not consistent over time. By breaking down crime and incarceration into two periods, 1980-86 and 1986-91 ... we find that incarceration rates rose by 65 percent and violent crime declined by 16 percent in the first period, but from 1986 to 1991, despite the fact that imprisonment rose 51 percent, violent crime also increased, by 15 percent. Clearly, no cause and effect relationship can be discerned here.[5]

One cannot necessarily accuse the NRA of collusion with "New Jack" economics, but certainly one can ask why this "Association" with its massive lobby is involved with such statistics in the first place. The NRA is not a law-enforcement agency, yet its insistence on the efficacy of these numbers has and will continue to influence the people who are shaping our public policy and who are accepting such findings uncritically. Its caricature of this information to support the pseudo-freedom of the second amendment holds the Constitution as a hostage par excellence. This ransom and trivialization of our deepest feelings of well-being enforce our worship of panic in which we are becoming the haters of our children and silent overseers of the suicide of our communities that fit now far too easily our superstitions of inconvenience, complexity, and incomprehensible unworthiness. Jefferson's statement, involving the double right to bear arms and of revolution, that:

"...The tree of liberty must be refreshed from time to time with the blood of patriots and tyrants. It is its natural manure..."[6] now appears as a tree but one of another mystery we cannot and do not know how to even name, and yet, as William Blake says in his epic poem "Jerusalem," such objects "freeze" our imaginations in the glow of their beauty and cruelty, until our nostrils and tongues and ears become globes of blood "...wandering distant in an unknown night."[7]

The third issue involves the hidden impulses behind our use of incarceration. We are engaged in a national seizure. We are throwing a whole generation of women and men into a form of confiscation that will leak out from behind the walls to demoralize and haunt us equally in ways that we cannot now anticipate or necessarily understand. The dissolution of our humanity in this moment of our history is solely our invention. We have presently 1.6 million women and men in prison, or 615 out of every 100,000 people. Our lock-up rate has gone up 40 percent since 1989. We resort to jail five to eight times more than most of the industrialized sister nations. African Americans are condemned at a rate more than seven times that of whites; 1,947 as compared to 306 per 100,000. Numbers from the Sentencing Project's most recent analysis entitled "Young Black Men and the Criminal Justice System: Five Years Later" tell us the story of an implacable advance. One out of three young black men are now under criminal justice supervision in one form or another, and in cities such as Washington, D.C., and Baltimore the toll has risen to more than

※ ※ one in two. The yearly price tag for corrections, police, and judicial and court costs (the justice system) has reached approximately a hundred billion dollars. The population of incarcerated African American males is 583,000. The number of African American males in the process of gaining a higher education is 537,000. Conviction for drug offenses accounts for 46 percent of the increase in sentencing since 1980. Comparisons in incarceration rates with other nations indicate that the length of sentence, rather than the number of people remanded to prison, is the primary determinant. Many experts conclude that alternatives to incarceration will have an impact, but nothing compared to altering sentencing time. Marc Mauer, in his essay "Americans Behind Bars," demonstrates that the practice of prison once implemented will last for generations. "Once prisons are built," he states, "they are in many respects a self-perpetuating entity. Prisons are constructed to last for 50–100 years, and their continued use over time contributes to a culture that makes their use seem logical and rational."[8]

If we look at the use African American males are coming to among us, despite the studies, congressional hearings, and task forces we are, in turn, staring at our own authorship of lethal violations that will incapacitate and ravish "us" as deeply as it incapacitates and ravishes "them." We cannot hope ever to recuperate from such a dimension of incalculable loss when we are, at the same time, mining that dimension and its grief for its supposed "riches." If this is the extension of the "logical and rational" of Mr. Mauer's reference, then the substance of our democracy seems at best an artificial pretext now to be quietly backgrounded and suffocated in order that a less obsolescent mecha-
※ nism might appear. The marketing of the disintegration of the African American community at the end of the twentieth century to guarantee

a "profitable" prison industry is a central squalor that can deposit us in a historical and social vacuum that will suck us dry. We are in the process of losing our communal abilities to tell ourselves the truths about our heritage of racist practice, its criminally historic intent, and how that intent banishes us to an already appeared future full of grotesque and pointless apathies rooted now so in ourselves that we can point to nowhere else for a precedent.

Napanoch was constructed between 1895 and 1900. Its castle-like fortifications are similar to the architectural styles of museums and asylums as those sister structures then also appeared on the American landscape. It was built in piecemeal segments by convict labor and opened on October 1, 1900. In 1984, when I first drove up to its entrance, I noticed the copper roofs of the turrets. Their cones were massive and gone deep green from 80 years of oxidation. The surrounding lawns and fields are the sites of sexual combat in the fall between male deer who come here to test themselves and their genetics. You can hear the dry, flat-clicked sounds as they lock racks at sunset, twist their heads and bodies in a Pleistocene dance at least 100,000 years old. The domestic cats that share this prison are scarred; muzzles ripped and bitten by rats, and they're jittery, feral. Bats sometimes get trapped in the long, dead, internal corridors, gliding from one end to another, never touching the endlessly mopped and scrubbed red-painted cement floors.

This prison had a riot in 1978. Hostages were taken. No one was killed. But there were injuries, and the one person who got stabbed was a teacher. "For an 'A' or an 'F,'" I wondered as I closed the door to my car. "And what am I doing?" The imposition of this building and its walls scared me then, and scares me to this day. I felt like I could hear those witches from Macbeth cackling out their incantations from the forgotten rafters where nobody's been for eight decades. Many years later when I taught Shakespeare, I'd get papers focusing on this king and his madness from inside the jailhouse I was about to enter, what kind of serial killer Shakespeare really imagined and brought into being who would make me ask myself on the most vulnerably unexpected levels who was teaching whom. I have a friend in charge of "civilian volunteers," such as myself, who began his experience by running, part-time, a literacy program training inmate tutors. Over the next few years, he would be given the full-time responsibilities of a first Cell-Study program, going from prison to prison. His position focused on one idea. If an inmate couldn't come to the areas designated for school, then the school would come to him. Whether a man was in solitary confinement or "key-locked" in his cell, my friend would go to him in order that he be able to carry on the studies that would bring him into literacy or a GED. During the period of that "Cell Study" program, my friend met an inmate, one he describes as a "profound teacher" who touched and altered his life. It was a conversation that began through an iron door, no faces to be seen, only voices heard. This man was a scholar of the Annales School of historical writing founded by Lucien Lefebre, Marc Bloch, and Fernand Braudel. It is a writing of history from the bottom up, beginning with landscapes, ecosystems, and patterns of trade. This prisoner directed my friend from Braudel's massive, three-volume history of capitalism to Immanuel Wallerstein's *The Modern World System*. Another teacher I share these experiences with started twenty-six years ago. He was in Quebec in 1970, teaching music at McGill University and performing with the Montreal Symphony, and had never heard of teaching in a prison. He interviewed for a job at the Wallkill Facility in Wallkill, New York. This site, constructed in the 1940s, was designed for model prisoners. The administration actually went out at that time canvassing other prisons around New York State for model prisoners. A trumpet player by trade, my colleague constructed a music program piece by piece, one man at a time. There was a large GED program and the beginnings of a new college experiment started by a local professor named Aaron Bindman. Students were introduced to basic theory and harmony. There was an atmosphere of deep seriousness from beginners to professional players down for drug problems. Some of those men have gone on to professional fame, while others continued their studies at outside schools and conservatories, eventually themselves to become teachers. The most profound discovery for this man was that the prisoners were "regular" people. The supposed hard-core, unredeemable men were often the ones most capable of the deepest personal feeling toward music and the change wrought by the making of art. That revelation came early for this teacher at Wallkill in terms of what he identified as the most basic kind of human change. At the same time, he, too, began asking questions, that would bring him unavoidable pain.

He has come to feel that a majority of prisoners are "down" because of lack of education and the destruction of the process of awareness that such an omission threatens and finally costs. At the time he taught, the rule of our color codes was the same "inside" as "outside," and though the cell blocks might be riven by racial bitterness, the music classrooms and their participants found a cohesion and authenticity that lay outside this conformity and sterilization. His strongest conclusion is that the study that comes with creativity introduced these men to a humanity they might otherwise never have been able to bring out of themselves. The musicians played on holidays, family days, and for the prison staff. They performed classical, modernist, and sacred pieces in chamber groups, mixed ensembles, and 25-piece stage bands. Never was there any disciplinary trouble, and out of hundreds of men who participated, only two or three returned to a life behind bars. Had I never had similar encounters, I would not have known quite what to think or feel. During the nearly ten years of my own experience, I came to know Platonic scholars, Sufi mystics, poets, Vietnam veterans, drag queens, and blues singers who would teach me and change me forever.

Chapter II
Masquerades

MY FIRST COURSES were preparatory and remedial. I had no idea at that time how my responsibilities toward these people would evolve and reappear. Over that almost ten-year period, I might teach a group of prisoners how to read and write and then see them through a Master's degree, depending upon the range of personal accomplishment and discipline. Because many of these men had never considered an education, especially the preparatory elements that I and others were then teaching, they were scared, and I was, too. I'd never stood before groups of people like this. They were knife- and gun-shot scarred. Hanger burns from self-inflicted tattoos covered hands and arms. Some were young, others middle-aged. They wore green, "prison green." Many had become weight-lifters, sat swollen from endless reps, at the combination desk-chairs of an institutional design they had abandoned years before for the life that would land them here.

They carried an anxiety you could smell–not sweat, but the grotesque menace of where they were. I didn't know that, either, in the beginning. What I did know is how they watched me, took me apart body sign by body sign. They were masters. The psychology of their predation and its impulses offered a calculation of risk and con-

cealment that was shattering, certainly for them, and for sure for whoever had been the object of this street expertise and its accumulation.
I felt then and I feel now that had I not somehow been "old" enough,
or had just the right number of duck feathers, I'd have been a mark
to be used and squeezed in ways that might have come to violate me
in an unexpected "later" when I was either ready or not ready; it would-
n't matter. It still might happen. One prisoner in a preparatory class,
confronted with an assignment to write a resumé, couldn't do it. The
impediment wasn't reading or writing. He had no skills other than
the ones he'd honed for himself as a "cat burglar." He asked if he could
write an essay, instead. I was never sorry about such improvisations.
Any habits or dependence upon some so-called technique had to be
junked every time you walked into a class-room.

That essay was an instruction manual. Concentrating first on surveillance. Watching the victim's town house or apartment for months,
knowing every crack in the near sidewalks, alleys, streets, and walls.
The garbage cans, dumpsters. When they were filled and when they
were emptied. Night or day. Start with that material. And then study the
humans. Neighbors, friends, local bag ladies, disoriented bums, services. Then the potential victims. Take apart their habits, their routines.
Mark them; trace them. Look for variations. Get a mental blueprint
of their days and nights. Who comes for visits, who doesn't. How many
windows. How many doors. Stand in alleys, sidewalks. Use the binoc-
ulars sparingly, only when it would matter. Look at clothes and jewelry
as those items were worn. All this done to avoid one thing. He showed
how you could be watched this way, twisted and sealed shut without
your ever knowing. He knew how fundamental and impersonal it was
and wanted others to know. It was one of the most beautifully crafted

process essays I'd ever seen. And it made me go almost numb. How such a former predator could snag you at the most subtle core, offer you a fancy little saucer of negation, that might invisibly chew at the edge of you for the rest of your life. Many had been responsible job-holders prior to their incarceration, many had been thugs of various practice, knowing nothing else.

The sanctuary of these instincts was as deeply necessary in the prison as it was in the street. But I discovered almost immediately another tension, one where these men were willing to let down their masquerade. Always there was a price to be paid. It could be peer ridicule, self-doubt, or the re-alignment with a past most had walked away from years before, when as promising young students in elementary or high school, they got pulled into the street and its criminal furies, never understanding how it would end in the repulsive, dead-in-life mirror that would strangle them far more deeply even than the subworld that had gotten them here.

I had taught English as a second language in New York City prior to moving to the Hudson Valley. In that situation, there might be in one class men and women from twelve different countries and cultures all with a yearning to learn. The formal approaches were not significantly different, except here I also concentrated on study skills and time management. I would hold a book in my hand and explain what it was, talk about its weight, its presence. Many of these people had no experience of books or the world a book might introduce, and they were suspicious, jammed by a new fright. Maybe that's because it wasn't physical. Really nothing physical could scare them. They'd been beaten, many of them since early childhood. The street with its brand of sudden death and reprisal was routine. Some, I later came to learn, had been locked in solitary confinement for up to two years. They could eat deprivation as some ritual coin, digest it and spit it back. It might get them beaten, their indeterminate sentences extended months and years.

A young black man on the streets of America in this moment of history stands a better chance of being violently killed than the soldier who slogged a sub-machine gun through the death-infested valleys around the real Ho Chi Minh Trail. But that same young man was unsure about a book, about me, about the act of volition that had placed him in a classroom buried in a penitentiary.

I had problems myself learning how to read which no one discovered until I was nine years old. I couldn't make out even the simplest two-letter preposition, such as "of." I memorized everything I heard, and managed to survive, but not well. The discovery came with a test, and then years of tutoring with a gifted woman whose specialty was learning disabilities, along with supplemental exercises directed by my mother, whose shock, reaction, and insistence probably saved my life. My affliction was called "word blindness" then. It's called all kinds of things now. It was three years before I began to learn how to read. I traced with my fingertips, endlessly, one word after another on a lap blackboard; and memorized by speaking each of those words out loud until I was almost nauseated with it. I don't really know what would have happened to me if that "test" hadn't come up, along with the two women who were there to push me, elevate me into a later nerve that would have been likely beyond my discovery. Some of my earliest childhood friends, Mexicans in the Southern California towns where we grew up, got wrapped in the heroin and gang violence and murder and now sit in prison or lie in a coffin. I've never forgotten that so-called disability. Even to this day it doesn't sit far away. With that I could probe, know the territory of an individual student's problem, attack it, and begin from that moment to show him a progressive journey into one newly learned skill after another. I came to understand that what separated myself from the men sitting in front of me were luck and my mother's absolute determination to make sure I could read— small elements of individual chance but ones nonetheless that do comprise a difference and that might bring us into meaning and how our fates hover there before both our uncertainties and fulfillments.

If I presented the "parts of speech," "similes and metaphors," "subject-verb agreement," I had to invent ways quietly to shock, look for tools, make those abstractions into things to be touched and held for specific examination.

Once, trying to explain the proposition of "metaphor," the model it might be for the process of thinking, the fact of it as an imagined thing, brought to but always lying just at the edge of substance, perhaps exciting the mind because of that into a sounding, I got stopped. If the thing finally lies as only a token of the real, although beautiful in all its systematic occasion, then what finally does inform it? So in that moment I looked around grabbed a prison garbage can full of half-sucked lollypops, slick potato-chips bags, cigarette butts, candy wrappers, and fruit gone semi-rotten. I peered at the class for one irreversible second and dumped that stunk garbage all over a table that fronted the room, painted a pale baby blue to ease the disturbances of mind floating in the air of that penitentiary. The prisoners stared, and gave me what seemed then a moment of silence. For whatever version of sanity I'd just lost in front of them, I never knew. But they giggled then, some of them letting their giggles descend into a deep compassionate laughter. I stood in my suddenly unveiled lunacy clinging to the empty can with one hand and holding the other in the air, and asked what it might be. One man said smiling, "It's the hand of a white man." I stared at him and at the white man's hand hanging there, barely able to embrace what I was about to do next. "No!" I almost screeched, "It's a metaphor. It's all a metaphor!" For the remainder of that first semester I would see men I didn't know, but obviously from other classes, look at me and shake their heads, wondering when the leftovers of this new instructor's mind were going to crawl out of the refrigerator. I realized then, if I could invent a "foolishness" out of which first realizations might appear, and never make it pat, that awkwardness might permit them a place to play and move before the foreignness of these books that must be read, these teachers to be brought into unconventional and finally lucid trust, especially before prison itself and its grotesque dulling. If I had to be Lear's Fool whispering "nuncle" to myself, in all the ways such whisperings could or could not be managed when that became necessary, I'd do that, too.

I showed these students (a counsellor for one of the other college programs, in a paper he'd written on prison education, called them "incarcerates") how to take accurate notes, how to increase memory and comprehension. I demanded they become experts with the dictionary. I began at this time to realize, too, that we as a nation are making specific segments of our population into a "teratology," monstrosities and deformations, and that the most sensationally publicized "criminals" are a "telling of wonders" that circumscribe and stalemate us. This "telling" is a transmission that ensnares us in new disciplines of hate, and as the "wonders" become more unusual in their spectacular confirmation, our present and future appear more falsified. The peo-

ple sitting in front of me were human in spite of the haze of teratolo-
gies wanting to choke this fact. I introduced these men to etymology;
how to trace a word in its life span from one interpretive element to
another. I timed them in class, offering them vocabulary to be uncovered so that when they went to this book they could do the work blind-
folded. If I pushed them to a limit nearly of breakage, forced a struggle
that at this earliest level disintegrated their feelings of impoverishment
before learning, before the presence of books, then they and I as their
teacher could come upon a beginning. I made them memorize the
"parts of speech," the definition of a sentence, a phrase. Overload was
always a shadow, but time was, too, and here they had to do two kinds,
that of their "sentences" and the other a "catch-up."

For some, this meant filling in the spaces between a disappear-
ance in the fifth grade and the scale of preparation now confronting
them that would mean the difference between their survival and failure when they began the actual college curriculum. The attitude of the
prison authorities comprised the most important, but often invisible
other half of the prison-education program's intent. In this case, the
Superintendent gave those men who were accepted into this chance
for a college degree the necessary time, meaning that this was their
program, their work to be monitored and followed. Without that cohesion nothing would have been possible.

I felt that an expertise with the parts of speech would break the
spell of their aversion and humiliation before those institutions, which
might, had they been more of an actual presence for these men at an
earlier age, have been the reason for them not going to prison. No one
has all the answers to these "what might have been" scenarios, and
probably no one has any of the answers. But maybe, if we have less

Education gives them dignity & humanity

tolerance for our superstitions and what ferments inside them, we can ask first questions about our shopping culture, what it's shopping for and whether or not we want these symptoms of the beginnings of its final stages. These are questions we deserve to ask ourselves.

I went from those early grammatical exercises to the composition of short written forms. Start with a paragraph. Explain what that is and how it works in relationship to the sentences inside it. Three or five or eight but make one. Then if the prepositions, or pronouns, verbs, or any other part of speech was causing ambiguity or incoherence, I could point to that anatomy, say, "Your preposition here in this sentence doesn't hold," or "The comparative form of this adjective is wrong." They'd know, and if not, then they had the tools to begin to struggle to know. It came hard.

With the memory of that unknown teacher with a stab wound in far away 1978, how would I grade these people? "F" for forensic breakthrough. My body marked by fine new creases. "B" for body double, the other me streaking out of my corporeal form with a "client" close behind.

I knew a prison psychologist who moonlit as a history instructor in the program. He was also a hostage negotiator. He told me about riots and that when I walked through the electric gates I had to know that the worst could happen. Carrying anything else besides this readiness in myself was a mistake I could not afford. I'd been through similar displacements on the outside. Working for a local newspaper, I uncovered a tragedy that involved a mining outfit. Its operation was shale, the kind found in the Catskills over 400 million years old. The mine heated the ancient rock in order to separate it from the liquids held inside it. The problem was the heating process. The filtration system for the stacks was almost criminally inadequate, and the fuels used for heating were toxic chemicals. In the higher temperatures of the required incineration, those chemicals underwent drastic uncontrolled change and became dioxin or sister-related dioxin compounds. The dioxin had spread all over a small, heavily populated valley, and the mine had done this burning for over two months. As the investigative reporter, I traced the fuel to a toxic dump site with a Mafia connection. It was a mess. One of the environmental organizations I contacted in Washington, D.C., said the chemicals used for the burning process constituted the most dangerous "witches brew" since Love Canal. I called the New York State Crime Commission in New York City and asked them about the "organization" that had supplied the fuels to this mine. In the middle of that conversation, I was asked if I had a wife and children. I said "yes," but what the hell did that have to do with the questions under discussion? The answer was, "Why don't you have your wife and kid go out and start your car in the morning for you." I didn't need an explanation after that.

But I wanted to know what my friend, the hostage negotiator, had to say. If I was unknowingly going to trip into ugly danger on the outside, that was one thing. I wanted here, on the inside, at least to be half-aware. He told me about the state of New Mexico's prison riot in the early 1980s, an incident with patterns of ghoulish violence and inner-prison reprisals nearly beyond description.

The anger that can hemorrhage in a prison is always lurking just at the edges of appearance. You can almost cut the air of it sometimes. It envelopes you like a rotten aquarium whose threat soaks the walls, the floor, and the skin. You can feel its waves pushing. For weeks after learning of this riot in New Mexico, I could barely go to work. My friend the hostage negotiator and scholar of Latin American history said this was the best kind of advice he could offer me, and it was. If I was going to go into these prisons, then I'd have to know in a worst-case scenario I could be taken. The men who seemed the most contained might be the ones, once unleashed, most capable of becoming beasts.

Those scenarios became a remote kind of hill in me, but one I had to watch. I told my friend about this, who said if I didn't have such a thing—not its armor, but its antenna—I would be at best a liability, a threat to the safety, first my own, and then others'. He was right.

It wasn't only the violence, either. The guards might be more dangerous than the prisoners. Many hated and resented the education programs, and hated the presence of instructors like myself. Late at night when leaving the depths of the prison, I'd see men shackled from ankle to neck escorted by three or four officers, the single man surrounded and the guards palming their night sticks just in case. In case of what? With the man in their charge tied like a trussed pig, who could know? Every day you see men, mostly non-white, shackled, wrists and shins locked and chain-joined, managing no more than a painful "duck" walk, the steel binding them flatly clanging.

That noise of chains grinds in after a while. Its ugly ceremony awaited the men carrying the same so-called dark "color" in slave ships and auction blocks, and the business of prison as it now enjoins new ranges of profit calls up these same stalemated images in a unity of historical abysses. With the apparatus of our pretenses, we can pretend that this closure of images does not exist.

The guards saw the "clientele" as "scum," and many wore thin surgical gloves, when prisoners had to be touched, especially after the

AIDS epidemic really set in. Most of the officers are white, from rural backgrounds. The majority of prisoners are black or Latino, in this case from New York City and other cities in the state. The mixture is filled with suspicion. Completely dependent upon the presence of these convicts for their jobs and benefits, guards hold their charges in the ugliest forms of contempt, but without them they would be economically helpless. The relationship perverts the dignity and humanity of both sides so profoundly that you can smell the lifelessness gushing out of it into a sphere of disqualification. If you are going to walk into it, you'd better see it, smell it. Let your senses start wandering in "... a distant and unknown night ... ,"[9] and they might never come back.

Chapter III
A Book of Iron

WHEN DE TOCQUEVILLE and his friend Gustave de Beaumont returned from their American journey, they composed "On the Penitentiary System in the United States and its Application in France." In April of 1844 before the Chamber of Deputies, de Tocqueville delivered a speech on prison reform. He pointed out that for the previous fifteen years the rising crime rate in France had been "extraordinary" and "alarming," and the rates of recidivism were even more "rapid." There is an application of both clarity and humanity in their suggestions. De Beaumont stated that,

> . . . Society has the right to punish but not to corrupt those punished. It is granted the awful power of killing the guilty; no one recognizes its right to deprave them. Everybody admits, however, that such is the pernicious influence of our prison system that whoever enters it half corrupted, leaves it completely depraved.[10]

De Tocqueville, in turn, in his address to the Chamber pointed out that one of the major issues confronting French society at that moment was an abyss it was poised on between its ideas about crime,

prisoners, and rehabilitation and the fabric of an imagination of a
civil body.

> You want to make him believe that he is incapable of ever raising
> himself, that the society into which he is going to return also believes
> only this; that it rejects him without respite or pity, that it endlessly
> pushes him toward crime! In a way you want to lock him in a legal
> hell from which there is no exit once it has been entered; you bind
> him to indescribable, implacable, and terrible fatality in which one
> wrong turn forbids a single step backwards! . . . But what have you
> achieved but a return to complete paganism? Don't the ideas which
> underlie all Europe's beliefs derive from the conception of possible
> rehabilitation . . . ?[11]

Questions such as these about the two countries he most loved tor-
mented de Tocqueville. He knew that our prisons in their nineteenth-
century versions of brutality had created an epidemic of insanity that
began in 1837 and did not diminish until 1840. The epidemic of insanity in the late twentieth century is outside the walls. Crime has become
our most peculiar and unlimited commodity, and through it we are
losing the constraints that allow us the fabric of our democracy, which,
in turn, allows us to remind ourselves how tenuous that fabric really
is. We are giving ourselves permission, and no longer is this process
gradual, to create forms of mass torture. Imprisonment is an act second only to killing itself. It is a display of the State's ability to degrade
absolutely, to institute a deployment of pain whose force is the latent
twin to what Nils Christie, in his essential analysis entitled "Crime Control as Industry," calls a ". . . new situation, with an unlimited reservoir
of acts which can be defined as crimes . . . also creates unlimited possi-

bilities for warfare against all sorts of unwanted acts."[12] This latent mass of novel commodifications implies the potential enslavement of populations yet to be born who are the reservoir of these acts in waiting. The "... new situation ...," as Christie calls it, should sicken and warn us, but it does not. Our media display pictures of so-called "maxi-maxi" prison cells, or torture chambers. They are also our most idealized embodiments of business and how business should be done.

I realized when I began teaching in the Prison Education Program that the stakes literally were for life or death. A man had to learn, to come to terms with a rigorous discipline. Each person knew his life depended on it. I think now after these many years that the stakes are the same for all of us. We do not know it like a prisoner does, and perhaps that is one of their gifts to us. I have never seen human beings struggle harder and with more courage for the accomplishments of mind than these prisoners over the period I worked with them, not only those who had a chance to end their "bids" and never come back, but those who will live out their lives and die there.

Corrections Today is the official publication of the American Correctional Association. It is filled with hundreds of advertisements from quick-draw construction outfits who can deliver a jail to a customer inside six months to portable x-ray machines I have personally seen that leaked all over the officers, visitors, and families of prisoners who were the subjects of this scrutiny. The families of the "raw materials" could receive too the leakage in this way, of our overabundance of punishment. A group of men, prisoners and former prisoners in in-house Master's programs, found that 75 percent of New York State's supply of bodies come from seven neighborhoods—Harlem, Brownsville, the Lower East Side, East New York, South Jamaica, the South

Bronx, and Bedford-Styvesant. Eighty-five percent of New York's prisoners are Hispanic or Black. One of those students, Eddie Ellis, a former director of community relations for the New York City branch of
the Black Panther Party, was convicted on a false murder charge and
spent 23 years in New York State's maximum-security prisons. Mr.
Ellis, now the co-founder and President of the Community Justice Center in Harlem, says the sojourn of African people has been one from
"... the plantation to the projects to the prisons ..." There is a chain of
certainties between Eddie Ellis's portrait of this "sojourn," *Corrections
Today* with its slick and shine format, and the seven neighborhoods.We
are moving toward a delivery of injury and pain by any means necessary.
Corrections Today is the Bible of Deliverance where you can find anything—"phones that enforce," free brochures from the "Human Restraint
Company," "Food Service" advertisements from "Aramark" who'll "...
customize a solution to meet your needs ..." But the raw material has
a face. At 8:30 in the morning those faces come into a classroom. You
watch their bewilderment before the parts of speech, the near anger
when they hear they'll have to take the necessary steps backwards to
find a "beginning," the hours of memorization they'll have to commit
themselves to amid the noise, danger, and array of extortions that compose their daily lives. You unknowingly have become one more form of
delivery in this system full of deliverance.

Except just this: the simple act of knowledge, the discovery of an
imagination of mind's shape stops the fulfillment of force either in
the present or future as those terms can be predicted by the view that
crime is our most unlimited natural resource. Here is an abundance
with the potential to give the industry based upon it to err on the side
of oversupply for what undesignated future to come who of us can

now know? Who sits before you are the "acts," though now in latency, as they were before birth, and now in "warehouse," as close as they can be to "after-dying," close as we can bring them to death. You can see with what ease these men can be projected as the saving bonanza they might truly be, and are close to becoming, and with equal ease how this abscess can be made to swell into the "sick breasts" of a new Covenant, to paraphrase the poet Robert Duncan in his "Where the Fox of This Stench Sulks,"[13] our industry sucking at the infection and we hoping that the safety of our distance won't leave us unprotected.

I stood up before these men on a day twelve years ago. They were having trouble with prepositions and the positive comparative and superlative forms of adverbs. I realized that this "trouble" they were having and my being there to help them with that "trouble," I and maybe eleven students, could bring this whole industry down. This was the making of another anatomy out of "parts," from what had now become a surplus and therefore dangerous population. I remember at that moment saying to them, "If you can get this, you'll put me out of a job." They smiled then and understood exactly what I meant. That was also the beginning of a trust that finally made me more "their" student than I could have ever known.

I worked the so-called lower division first, preparatory, then freshman and sophomore courses. One of those prisoners was as tall sitting down as I am standing up. He was a graceful man who had had a scholarship to play basketball. Lost it all to drugs. Now he was having problems with basic grammar. I was almost afraid to sit next to him, go through his "sentences." The use of that word was hard to breathe out. Its implications, until then not wholly considered, became self-consciously present. A sentence is as far as a breath can be carried, as a sentence is as far as a life can be condemned. Your sentences, Wilbert, are incoherent. They don't make any sense. How to locate one starting act from these ruins, get them to see it, however awkwardly, and climb from that one personally constructed accessible rung. It might take half a semester and in some instances a preparatory course repeated more than once to get through all the background of irritation, malice, and suspicion many of these men carried from a previous experience of "school."

It was a process of memorization mixed with a constant practice of writing, correcting, dictionary work, and study skills. No slack. No short cuts. Senators like Jesse Helms hated these programs. There was so much misunderstanding and basic incomprehension that any question about the "abilities" of these men could bring disaster. Often the faculties of the sponsoring colleges themselves looked upon their own programs as "inferior" and the prisoners as a question, although most of these teachers never walked through the "gates" to find out.

I taught a course in eighteenth-century British literature. The majority of the students were able to control the materials. One man, however, who had received consistent "A's" from teachers in former courses, handed me a final essay. The piece was a disaster. He had plagiarized. There was hardly one coherent sentence. Even the most basic grammatical construction was nearly non-existent. I gave the man an "F" after a number of warnings over previous sloppy and thoughtless drafts. Two weeks later I got a call from the president of the faculty senate of the sponsoring state college questioning my grounds for the grade.

Doubt about grades and how such fixed portraits might influence and alter the lives of students are essential. These judgements, whether positive or negative, can end up being a prosecution in themselves, and for myself, in this position of teacher, I try never to tease that authority. A, B, C, D, and F are measurements required by the university, and if they are to be used as such currency, teachers at all levels must be deeply aware of their ambiguities. The student had written the faculty senate citing the excellence of his academic record, and what he believed to be a racial prejudice on my part. How with all his "A's" could there be an "F"? I said the materials spoke for themselves, that there had been specific and prior warning about the on-going lack of quality in the work throughout the semester.

I was questioned about my qualifications, my ethics, and told the case under consideration might be taken to another level. I asked then about this man's "A's" and what such grades meant about those members of the faculty this person represented who'd given these gifts and whether or not a major breech had taken place. I inquired, too, whether or not a "review" was as equally necessary for them as it appeared to be for me. I felt strongly then and feel as strongly to this day that such a prisoner and the teachers who had given him his delusional "grades" endangered all the men in the Prison Education program who struggled desperately in the majority of instances for the foundations that might free them and offer them the choices by which they had a chance never to come back. One tragedy could be used as a "Willie Horton" issue, poisoning all that the others had accomplished legitimately and beyond doubt. Continuous public hatred and superstition, a prosthetics co-equal in its "acts in waiting" to crime itself, shadowed every grade, every painful motion forward toward renewal, the years I was there for the cheapest, most humane form of rehabilitation yet devised.

A significant part of those first few years was spent working with Vietnam War veterans. They were my contemporaries. I did not go to

this war. I had no deferments. I refused induction into the armed services, a felony that put me also on a journey toward prison and to be
tracked down by the FBI. At one point in my personal turmoil over
the Vietnam War, I stayed with a Quaker family in an isolated valley of
the Nevada desert. The father, still then in the midst of a life-long med-
ical practice, had been himself a conscientious objector in the Second
World War. He had been assigned alternative service as a doctor outside of Fresno, California, in districts that were then still very rural.
But word got around that because he was an "objector," that somehow equated with "spy," and one night as he was going on house calls
he was taken. His wife and their then young son, my close friend,
received an anonymous call. Told the father was in a barn and was
going to be lynched, they set out on a frantic drive to try to save him.
The barn, surrounded by the dark shapes of cars, was open. They found
him standing in a circle of men, with a noose literally half-tightened
around his neck. This doctor, normally a quiet man, had an eloquence
in himself that had saved his life up to that point. When the mother
and young son walked into the midst of this crowd and pulled the
rope down from the rafters before them, the about-to-be lynchers dis-
persed. The woman and boy grabbed the father, the husband, and on
the way home she descended into a nervous breakdown. My appearance in this valley brought up not only these memories, but the tragedy
of their son, my friend who'd taken me there to hide, to think, who
had himself been a conscientious objector, then in a sudden episode
of doubt over whether he could have been as strong as his father, good
enough for the "objector's" task, joined an army combat unit.

I have four uncles who fought in previous conflicts. Two participated in the Spanish Civil War in the Abraham Lincoln Brigades and

distinguished themselves in this controversial and ugly rehearsal for the Second World War. Another fought the Japanese in the South Pacific and forever after suffered from the grenade wound not only to his body and mind, but periodic attacks from the malaria he contracted at Tarawa or Kwajalein or any of a number of death zones where he and others spilled themselves. The last uncle went from a ranch in Wyoming to the theaters of Europe, experiencing non-stop combat for years. That uncle, one of my favorites, used to take me fishing when I was a boy off the coast of Santa Cruz, California, where he had become a fireman. There I'd watch this gentle man fall into silences, and smoke, one pack after another that I even knew then contained memories that had no words for their images. I didn't ask. It wasn't that I knew better. There was no hushed pool of meanness awaiting my questions. I was his nephew, and what I could do was bait his lines or open his beers with a church-key and spend afternoons that way watching the seals take our catch—be a kid and make him laugh.

Those uncles fought to save their lives and mine. My father was a Jew, a farmer given a crucial deferment to grow food during the terrible years of "The War," as they called it. My mother was a mixture of Indian/Mexican and Welsh ancestors, first settlers of the Americas on both sides, redwood and Sequoia lumberjacks who came to take the land for its fortunes. Had the Nazis won, either of those contaminants would have condemned me, if not to immediate death, then to an Aryan version of slavery. The Vietnam War split my family as it did so many others, split cherished memories and tendernesses that can never be gotten back. Some of those beloved uncles could not and would not look at me over my stand against this war. If they had been Jews and could have sung the Kaddish over me, they would have.

I stayed with that Quaker family in Nevada, and their son who was then and still is a park ranger. I considered going to British Columbia to become an expatriate, but climbing a high mountain one day I looked out over the magnificent Great Basin Desert, watching the golden eagles circling above me, and stopped thinking about going anywhere other than where I stood. I got a train out of Milford, Utah, and came home, if it had to contain prison, too. My stand often convulsed me to the edge of sicknesses I had never known, nor would ever want to. The contempt some of my beloved uncles felt for me wounds me to this day, and my boyhood friends who went to the jungles of Asia to die or come back somehow, are still my friends.

I could not have known how the men I knew, who fought this war only to end up wasting another part of their lives warehoused in prisons where I taught, would bring this material to a painful surface again and at the same time, by their presence and courage to live, even in the grotesque hells they are condemned to, present a whole new set of questions about who I am, and what is to become of their nation, because although they spilled their guts and finally their sanity, it is theirs, too, and ours as they are a part crucially of our wished-for throwaway selves. The grief, bewilderment, and unreality of the Vietnam War seems to have a doubly invisible fate—that of its original distance and unattached menace, and now, for a catastrophic number of those veterans, a confinement in our prisons that comprises a reincarnation into a second and even more dangerous invisibility. Each one of these men places the framework of our democratic/industrial institutions, and their production of both profit and indifference, in suspension. Our basic administered immunities before them and their mental illnesses are issues that, as part of the sum of our numbnesses, pervert and sicken us as they were perverted and sickened themselves. They, too, are an essential part of the deformations we can identity as our new raw materials. In combination with indifference as the purest managerial element of our technical machinery, we are hurling ourselves toward sinister accomplishment and a Book of Iron that will enable us to move more freely into the drastic tasks which lie ahead. The Vietnam War in all of its anguish has become a clinical description for our actuarial abysses and what they ultimately might serve.

This Cold War made us cold, and like the Ahania in Blake's terrifying book, we have become "unbodied" and "parted" in our civil conception of selves. The numbers game surrounding Vietnam War veterans remains for us a series of disembodied revelations that we have never managed to touch or be touched by. There is something staggering in this. The possibilities that these numbers represent the convulsed evocations of our undoing, that they may be the initial ground where our post mortem futures are now appearing, and that we feel nothing before them other than as an episode gradually to be sunk into the "unmentionable" of our present politics, is almost ghoulish in its portentousness. There were 58,000 killed in this war. There are to this date 130,000 to 150,000 suicides among its veterans. A significant percentage of those who experienced actual combat have since, in turn, experienced the incomprehensible loss to prison of their most potentially active and creative years as adult males in our society. What they could have been is for someone else to say. What they are now, however, may be an essential act of identification for who we are, and where we are, if we are not to be smothered in the prosperities of our wanton unawareness. Their service, too, is a double fate, the one for the armed forces where they served their country, and, now, the service for "time" where they serve the corrections industry in what may be a far more vital role for their nation and its economy, no matter the cynicism and threat shadowing all "New Jack" profit margins.

Every word here in this place is a pliant vacuum that can swim or fly, form or unform at will of the cravings that cling to it. For instance, "bid" unfolds through the labyrinth of this pit. "Bid" is a reference to sentencing time, the dead portion of existence each prisoner plea-bargains for in return for a confession—not necessarily for what was actually done but for what the offender and prosecutor have agreed about what will be revealed before the court, not to insure justice but the acceleration of sentencing. The Constitutional safeguard of fair trial is employed as a threat. If the accused uses the safeguard and loses, the sanctions against her or him will be increased. If you're from one of the "throw-away" populations, you get a "throw-away" lawyer, too. The bargain basement is all inclusive. "Bid" is also a reference to both the production of crime and the production of control. These industrial twins have an absolute no-limit growth principle; "service" on all levels, no matter how much our surplus populations may attempt to avoid it, in relationship to its function promises an endless competition for all the highest "bidders," those who serve and those who do the servicing for the unmeasurable billions and their sullen whirlwinds.

Everywhere I turn when I think of numbers in relationship to the Vietnam War, there is another bewilderment. In March of 1993 when the population of our prisons approached one million, 200,000 of those bodies were veterans of this geyser head of malignancy and inertia. What does that number signify, and even in wanting to ask such a question do the persons at the center of de Tocqueville's address—you and me, the ones supposedly capable of sustaining community, who hold the life of the Bill of Rights in the palms of our hands as if it were a fallen nestling knowing that's how frail its life really is—become shadows lying outside the public and private trusts that the author of "Democracy in America" saw as central to the condition of our fulfillment? In the face of these numbers, can we any longer be trusted with the life of these words and what they ask us to consider? For me, the ugliness of these questions begins in part with Vietnam. If the core of our now expertly tuned disinterest is the image and reality of prison, then a substantial segment of the core of prison itself as it exists in all its product capacities is Vietnam.

One of the veterans I knew came back from Southeast Asia and couldn't stop killing. He suffers from Delayed Stress Syndrome. He committed a particularly messy strangulation murder and is in prison for life. He is sick. Yet he is one of the most humane men I have ever known. When this prisoner first New Jacked, he was a member of the Aryan Nation, as dangerous a racist cult on the inside as the outside. Much of his transformation is directly attributable to his attempt to gain a higher education. I was assigned a beginning composition and rhetoric course. Some of the men there had a fine control of grammatical and rhetorical mechanics; some didn't. "Nick" was struggling. He was trying to find a way to master both the formal research essay, the final object of the course, and the formal presence of the English language. Two weeks into the course, I interviewed each student to discover their personal directions and interests, and Nick asked if he could do his essay on the M16. My habit was to review all research papers on a step-by-step basis throughout any given semester to make sure the process was being clearly formulated and exercised. For every student, including Nick, it was an exacting, often frustrating labor. His material came in bits and fragments at first, slowly building. But the arrangement soon took on a shape where both his language and his thinking found an increasing surety over terrain on which the whole weight of this war's deformation continues to fall. His essay offers himself and us—from the inflexible evasions and blanknesses that hover over it—no rescue.

The introductory segment of the piece focused on the M16's evolution from the M1, the assault rifle of World War II American forces. This weapon was mocked in the recent media coverage of Haiti, as part of the outworn arsenal of Haitian troops. But our own army wanted those weapons, wanted them badly. They knew what the M1 could and can do. As one kind of killing machine, even though heavy, it was superb for its time. In the late forties and early fifties, the army began the attempt to develop a fully automatic, light-weight, rapid-fire assault rife because Mikhail Kalashnikov's AK47 made everything that had gone before it obsolete. Those experimental prototypes included the T25, the M14, and the AR10 with its impressive but problem-ridden design. In late 1957 Eugene Stoner, one of the greatest modern small-arms designers, was completing the first test models of his AR15 with its aluminum alloys and plastics and weight of 6.13 pounds. It needed no lubrication, was impervious to dust, rust, and extreme cold, and its tumbling small-caliber bullet delivered fatal, horrifying wounds. In the summer of 1960, when General Curtis LeMay saw what the rifle could do, he personally sought permission to order 80,000 for his own Air Force ground troops. The AR15 made the M14, the army's weapon of choice, into an instant antique. Yet army ordnance officers, insisting the AR15 fit their specifications, began to tinker with Stoner's rifle, and the result was the M16. In 1966, after troops in Vietnam carrying the M14 had been cut to shreds, army ordnance ordered a slow-burning ball powder for the M16, knowing this propellant would leave a residue. An M16 rifle with this powder posed for the trooper carrying it in battle a deadly incomprehension everywhere it was used. The pattern of Nick's essay not only discussed these origins of the M16 but gave a detailed analysis of its parts, its design, and how those factors directly translated into an object held in the hands of a young man who would have depended absolutely upon this object for his life.

Nick's assessment has been crucially left out of our nation's self-knowledge. The M16, during those years, often failed for individual troopers under the conditions for which it was supposedly designed. Our army sent the men who used it during this time into battle with inadequate and confusing maintenance instructions. The common foot soldiers on the line, frantically desperate, began mail-ordering rifle lubricants, solvents, shoe strings, WD-40, and insect repellents to clean their pieces. The defects, which were known, were either overlooked or ignored by those officials who should have been responsible. How the men who would get chewed out of their lives, however, fit into this scenario proposes another image, one of whole platoons discovering in the midst of fire-fights that down to a man their weapons jammed, became worthless. Soldiers, ours, lay dead next to M16's that had been broken down; in their panic and helplessness they had been shot, stabbed, left as offerings to the junk that had castrated their existence.

The extremities of terrain, climate, and the individual soldier's ability to keep a piece functional are all factors of survival. But that soldier's ability, no matter how expert, could have never overcome the forces that lay behind this weapon's documented failure. By the time the army itself admitted the real problem, over 89 million rounds had been fired with this propellant, and no one to this day knows how many of our soldiers' lives were lost to the residue build-up in their M16s. In May of 1967, the Ichord Congressional Committee was formed to investigate what had happened. After extensive inquiry, it found, among a number of other revelations, the malfunctions were directly attributable to the ball propellant produced by Olin Mathieson, which had a close relationship to high-ranking officers in army munitions, weapons, and materiel commands. In addition, high-ranking Department of the Army officers were aware of the ball propellant's adverse effects on the rifle; and finally, the army's rifle program management bordered on criminal negligence. The complicated history shadowing this "negligence" included not only a contempt for the common draftee on the part of the army, but the speechlessness still surrounding the Ichord Committee's last findings that at last resolved nothing. Such resolution was left for the troopers themselves, who went into the field expecting the weapon not to function and who because of that expectation carried extra bolts.[14]

Why bring up these issues again? Why not let these freaks stay where they are, hidden from the rest of us until their freakish stories slide into historical silence that by that suffocation makes even more convenient the bribing of our amnesia? It is certainly one thing to send children to war; that is a cruelty in itself always standing outside what we can ask ours or any other language to do, to patch injury that can find no breath to speak with. To send them to war with a weapon that stands a good chance of not working is an abyss that falsifies the deepest mournings and sorrows that would allow us a passage. Such an apparatus has bred a system of excuses and paradoxes transcending the continuities and even discontinuities that have formerly given us the participatory identities we must daily imagine and call into being. Those paradoxes now are almost in themselves a metaphysics, and we can barely discern any longer what language will act against it, what language will not be struck dumb.

As I composed this essay in Norman, Oklahoma, the former Secretary of Defense, Robert McNamara, revealed at that moment how little the actual living life of the nation mattered to him and to those around him. Perhaps in some someday when we have a language fixing us to Earth again beyond the present encumbering fetters, we'll be able to fit, however awkwardly, this material into place where an alphabet of trust can re-emerge and each of those vowel and consonantal parts will be necessary to each other once more. What rage or anguish can help us to enunciate even the beginnings of a saying of what cannot be said to men who secretly, and as we know now, deliberately snare existence into an ocean of death sweat, and then have the rest, unknowingly, outside of any knowing we could ever, in the trust we gave them, want or come to, slurp as deeply as they from it? Those actions impose upon us a traumatic obscurity and have become the vehicle of our mutual abandonment, and our violating paralyses.

At that moment also, in Oklahoma, the further symptoms of such betrayal had now suffocated the life of the nation at a new level. The Alfred P. Murrah Federal Building in Oklahoma City along with the human beings who were inside it had been so massively destroyed by civil violence that the integrity of appearances we all rely upon for the ground of our daily lives seems to have been incalculably swept aside. The revelation that the men who may have committed such acts are young, uneducated, white members of militias, paranoiacally arming themselves against conspiracies by their government, can find finally no point of arbitration. The coldness, cruelty, and appetite for wrath these grievances propose drip into the wounds of our common unrealities that form at least part of a truth. The real betrayal by those men in power whom we entrusted with our lives has produced an existence so tentative for some that they now carry their own unimaginable sums of toxic consequence, and we, the others who do not want to be as deeply broken, will go on being broken nonetheless if we do not have the courage properly to retrace the backgrounding shadows of our demoralization. Such lethal shadows of our existence have produced a pathology so remote there is no prosecution or punishment that can give us, the living, wholly back the imagination of our desire to be alive from those who would in an infected completeness concentrate upon an impulse to die and bring us into their order of death. These are the crystallizations of the private properties of self that in their demonic extremity fulfill de Tocqueville's most perilous warnings about the collapse of both our private and public worlds and the "fatal tendency" of racism threatening our eighteenth-century wishes from beginning to potentially end in "strange vicissitudes." If we are to go on providing ourselves with the means to our traditional violence, then at some moment those traditions will move beyond any boundary we presently know or understand, and in that instance we might enter into the preparatory unrecognition of a more drastic ideological remove and civil suicide that has, up to this time, floated around us as entertainment. The will to power through rumors of conspiracy, in its subverting viciousness, asks us to disown what potentialities we hold in the actual trust there is left to us, and substitute a ruling numbness. It is part of the ordination of care-lessness equal to, if not greater than, McNamara's authorship of the reduction we have been forced to live through and its dictatorial prince-dom that has perverted our lives. If the worship of individuality throws up an autonomy this distorted, whether a Timothy McVeigh or a Robert McNamara, then where in any of our traditions do we have the chance to reimagine who we are and where we are before the hunger of this identity and the ends it wants and must have?

How does a man such as Nick regain his humanity, and in a New York State maximum-security prison is this even possible? I knew other prisoners in his cell block, Black men who eventually distinguished themselves in the Master's program primarily because of Nick. They witnessed a transformation beginning from Aryan warrior. They needed his help to learn to read and to write. He was the only one on that cell block they could go to.

The process of teaching another human being at this level under these circumstances—to offer that person a scale by which a personal existence is no longer enfeebled by the anaesthesia and estrangement that ravish and ultimately bring a person to prison, to the mechanics of degradation warehousing means—is to enter a sphere of vulnerabil-ity where the apparatus of falsification, primarily racist falsification and its pretenses, is loosened from the roots of its consolidation. The men I came to know over these years had only one thing left: their minds. All other formula of normality had succumbed to the official distances a down time transpires into, something so personal you can feel it soaking, pulsing, a violating angel in waiting no one ever can let come to him.

Where can we propose a counter-motion to the private and public realms of carelessness that impose upon us stagnations so immense that carelessness itself through its organized negations becomes a skill? More essentially, where to start? Nick was able to dissolve these manipulating crusts that mark every one of our lives with a remove. The bond at this primary level leaves no room for anything but its own encounter, and parasitic, automatic codes for "teacher" and "student" begin to crumble. "Teaching"—and I don't know if this word can adequately fix the details of risk before the collapse of personal existence in a prison, to make this one remaining human organ come into a life one person at a time—brings you slowly into a realization of the historical barrenness in which we are so deeply sealed and that we could be, if we were not the food (to paraphrase Blake's "The Sick Rose") of the invisible worm, finding our beds of crimson joy, a people awakening beyond the starvation that humiliates and frames us in the drudgeries of an enforced end, one beckoning us on the outside to a time as ugly in its punishment as the minutes and seconds on the inside.

Nick immersed himself in a study, one without ease, got his Bachelor's degree but refused to go on to a Master's. He continued tutoring others up to the moment of his prison transfer, changing the lives of the men who came to him for help. In this process, in the terrible extremity of prison he recast himself in a quiet, unassuming rectitude, and in that helped to recast the men who would go on to similar achievement. There were a number of prisoners I knew like Nick, men who will never get out but who matter essentially because through them the less drastically condemned can step outside the supervisory forces of peer pressure and the systemic ridicule that work to strip them utterly of even the most minimal adulthood—a minimum where your teeth, your body, the smallest daily functions disappear into the routines of "security."

I met "Kenneth" in a creative-writing course. He was down a second time. Armed robbery. He'd been in the Americal Division, the same one Lieutenant William Calley belonged to, the officer responsible for the My Lai massacre where 347 civilians, primarily women and children, were murdered by American troops in 1968. Such incidents, in a war where the enemy had no believable identity, were more often than not the rule. Though Kenneth said he did not participate in the massacre, he became sickened over the constant killing and refused finally to go into the field. He was thrown into the Long Binh Jailhouse, known to the grunts sentenced there as "LBJ," a short distance northwest of Saigon. Kenneth was black, from New York City. When I met him in 1986, his two bids had already added up to fifteen years. The first cage in Vietnam he couldn't stand, so he went back into the killing. Back home, on the verge of killing still, he armed himself for robbery. The simplicity of the equation is an injury, and though hidden, exists still as a central impoverishment. Why? Kenneth found a measure for the consequences he'd lived through and composed the finest beginning poetry I've ever seen.

Creative writing for me is one of the most difficult courses. How do you teach this or any art? Whether the form is poetry or prose, can you as a teacher compel your students toward what is a living matter at work in a language? I try to propose an approach to a writing workshop based upon two intersecting stages. The introductory stage is a preparatory reading. I use this as not only an element of suggestion to be built upon, but as an assemblage of background information that might move a student toward the permission necessary for writ-

ing that probes existence and might tell a reader why so many lives
have been risked for nothing more than words made of breath and
the worlds that have fallen together or apart because of those pres-
ences. For this course I introduced the works of H.D. (Hilda Doolittle),
William Carlos Williams, Ezra Pound, Charles Olson, Robert Duncan, and Mari Sandoz. If an individual student wanted to explore materials beyond these basic foundations, then further names and titles
could be given, and often I personally went to the libraries myself
since the logistics posed between prison and the outside made access
too slow. Through H.D., for instance, because of her susceptibility to
the awareness of existence around her, and her musical precision, I
could go to a poem by George Herbert or Sappho, showing how a
poet thinks with living things and their details and how those details
have a weight and energy that make the world either alive or dead.
The act of reading might carry a nearly equal movement. The second
stage was a rigorous examination of process through questions that
might take the men in this course beyond liking or disliking the works
offered or even beyond the ornaments of self-expression. This examination focused on some of the following questions I felt might offer
a stronger concision in terms not only of how those students might
approach their own works but also, beyond the course, how they might
approach any living literature.

What are concrete data, opposed to decoration?

How does a music fall on the simple spoken word?

Is the work an accurate transmission of what is seen, felt, or heard,
and what pushes its movement?

What is artistic conviction, and how does it appear?

What is the poem or fiction as an emotional object that commands both feeling and intelligence?

How does an actual living witness in writing direct itself toward an instance of ordered music in a poetic line or prose sentence?

How is an image made of sight, touch, taste, and smell?

What is dead verse or prose, poor verse or prose, and why? What is the weight of a single word and its sensory fulfillment in poetry or prose?

The above examples are only some of the questions I posed in my workshop in order to suggest what reservoirs of risk and thought lie behind the art. The discovery of such an inquiry is based not only on my experience as a novelist and poet but on the experiences of other writers, such as William Carlos Williams, Louis Zukofsky, Robert Duncan, Gertrude Stein, and James Baldwin. What comprises the foundation of teaching, and, in this time where there is so much loss, does it matter that I or any other artist might want to teach? For myself, the answer is always a difficult "yes."

Chapter IV
Nerve Endings

IN AUGUST OF 1994, President Clinton's Crime Bill destroyed the monies designated on a nation-wide basis for all Prison Education programs. The Federal or Pell Grants were for books; without books, like it or not, there are no programs. Those monies constituted less than one percent of all federal funds designated for higher education and were beginning to offer proof, at least in the program of which I was a part, that this form of rehabilitation might be the cheapest, most far reaching yet devised. For a man like Kenneth, these programs opened up a new world and offered a restoration of chances, not just for himself personally, but for ourselves. He literally devoured the readings offered to him, as if they were the nutrient he'd been waiting for, and began asking for compilations of myths, stories, and legends that would demand further study. He went to William Carlos Williams' *Imaginations* in hopes of finding direction. His collection of first poems based on his experience as a "grunt" in Vietnam offers little comfort. Instead, what is given is a transmission so deeply formed and composed that the reader becomes inextricably shadowed by the living arrangement of things which at once possess and bind us to their crisis:

At times

       trees

            resemble so much

                 nerve endings.

                      Fleshy,

                 raw exposed

          seems inevitable

       they'll blow

someday

         This thing about honor, less clearly defined:

Honor is the

       sight of red-gray matter

           sickly falling

                in small jellied

clumps

       from the waist

          of a mango tree

              II

          like opaque snot

                sliding off

9th century

       china.

         Honor is ...

There is no ornamentation here, nothing unnecessary. The detail of parts, the breath-by-breath construction of the poet's awareness and how he directs this language toward an actual act of seeing and how that act attracts reality, offers us no escapable device. At the same time, through his rigor, he sounds out "This thing about honor" far more intimately than the policy arrangements of an "honor" that brought him to stand inside the "sickly falling" clumps of his and our condition of shattered minds that can think up no more than an industrial future whose central jewel is prison. Kenneth also anticipates and answers Robert McNamara, who in *In Retrospect* says, ". . . Obviously there are things you cannot quantify: honor and beauty, for example . . ."[15] McNamara's precious order and distance become an even more realized distortion before the account of this poem and its beauty of first consequences that cannot be impeded, nor will it succumb to the lures of the obvious where a whole geography, to the men who had to slog through it, became known as the "slab."

Often have wondered

     how NVA treat captured

         beyond print, and the

11th brigade

   was on

      Red Mountain

        less than three days

         found members

  of an ambushed

    squad

staked to the ground,

bound

hand & foot

left by

departing

NVA regulars

who had neither time

nor-

to deal

with captured GI's;

admonished them

tucked them away

for safe keeping

fate's a bitch

ain't it?

the grunts laughed.

Kenneth wrote about these poems, "I'm attempting to discover what LINE is, what SYLLABLE is supposed to be; the above is a reflection of the exploration. I think I do very much want to write, but my problem is separating ideas from things—and where does the medium lie, for the sake of poetic creativity, between those extremes?" Perhaps, in hoping to "tuck" this man, and others like him, in a penal banishment, we can contrive relief, or failing that, the vague symptoms of reassurance that instruct us that Kenneth's presence and worth as a man doesn't matter. His poems tell us, however, about a vacuum of contrivances and dismissals that rule us in their despoil.

I was asked once many years ago why I taught in a prison, what secret in myself made me go there. Maybe it was that long-ago grandfather or uncle haunting me, my own near brush with prison because of my refusal to go to Vietnam, or maybe I was afraid of this portrait I'm trying to write, knowing before any "knowing" could appear what it might be. If Kenneth, before our present compulsive retributions, is truly "surplus," then we are in what the American Correctional Association calls, in its spring, 1997, marketing service notice, ". . . this extraordinary market . . ."

> The corrections industry continues to grow at an unprecedented rate. With the number of inmates incarcerated in our nation's prisons, jails, and detention facilities approaching 1.5 million, the need for technological advancement in the development of new products and services continues to be an industry priority. This growth translates to an unlimited opportunity for your company to profit from this multi-billion dollar industry. Let ACA help you tap into this extraordinary market.

> The ACA's 127th Congress of Correction will take place August 10–14, 1997 in Orlando, Florida. The 1998 Winter Conference will be held January 19th & 20th, 1998 in San Antonio, Texas. These events, the largest of their kind in the world, will heighten your company's visibility to the corrections marketplace. *Corrections Today* magazine, ACA's international publication, reaches out to thousands of decision-makers at all levels. June's issue, "Young Offenders: A New Breed," will explore how the juvenile justice system and adult facil-

ities are reexamining how they need to handle these younger care-free offenders. Additionally, ACA's direct mail services will help you put your materials into the hands of specific target groups.[16]

We do not know what the long-lasting infection of "... the extraordinary market..." will do to us, especially a "market" culture with this large an investment. In my home state of New York, for instance, when Mario Cuomo began his series of governorships in 1983, there were 39 prisons and 26,499 prisoners. In the year of his defeat, 1994, running for what he thought would be a fourth consecutive term, there were over 64,000 prisoners and 69 prisons. Did this man, with his supposed moral stand against the death penalty, bribe an electorate primarily in favor of death penalties with a glut of prison construction? Did he use these constructions to legitimize the morality of his personal blockage of the death penalty, and what did he and ourselves receive in the exchange? Mario Cuomo is responsible for the appearance of more new prison space than all previous governors combined in New York State's history. He is the Prison Builder. What "morality" was behind the subordination of a death penalty? Can 30 new prisons be the act of conscience by which the State of New York absolved itself from a degradation that falsifies and replaces democracy with a purchase that so threatens democracy itself at its core? The man who originally warned me about prison, the attention you must pay every second you're on the "inside," warned me also about the death penalty. It wasn't direct. It was more a warning about myself, about what can happen to you on the inside if you're there long enough between uniforms, the prisoner "greens" and the guard "blues" as a civilian. The cynicism that can catch hold, insulate you without your knowing it, the ugly silent pain you think won't necessarily soak into you since you're the one who can slide through the mirrored electronic gates. The death penalty's everywhere in a prison. The grotesque spit-shined corridors reek with it. Time is dead here. The one who enters this space of "dead time" and its marginalities goes dead legally and civilly; the only object left to lie in wait is the body itself. One of the prisoner's essays on inmate suicide cites "McKinney's Consolidated Laws of New York State Annotated" to confirm the exact nature of this "deadness":

> ... a sentence of imprisonment ... having a minimum of one day and a maximum of life, forfeits all the public offices, and suspends, during the term of the sentence, all the civil rights, and all the private trusts, authority, or powers of, or held by the person sentenced.[17]

"McKinney's" interpretation uses the terms of the verb "to suspend" in its most depravational sense: "... to lose the exercise of a function ..." Get riveted to this space, and you lose your function as a human being. Upon release, however long that takes, if you can remember what your function was, its daily smallest details apart from what took its place, then probably you weren't really "alive" while you were "dead." Maybe it can be compared to a stroke where your only chance to recover is through repetition therapy, reawakening the most overlooked details between the "before" and "after" person who, in nearly becoming ancestral, never got the benefits of the full evaporation. If you're white and middle-class, and you're thrown into this nether world, the suspension can slowly become an "invitation," as the prisoner's startling essay on suicide stated, "... to transform existence ..." by getting not a new or old one, but just a life, back from what swallowed it up whether it's in the world of shades or not. The question of being, of transformation itself, is posed by another inmate, a prisoner in a college program at Attica, written under the pseudonym "Bukarin" in 1988:

> I cannot take it anymore
> This pain inside I can't ignore
> It tears my mind in a million parts
> And I cannot stop it once it starts
>
> The visions haunt me while I sleep
> Inflicting wounds that are so deep
> An agony no one can see
> Because it's locked inside of me;
>
> I cannot take this anymore,
> The pain inside has won the war
> And now this silver blade of steel
> Will rid me of the pain I feel.

The reference both to personal loss and to a collapse of worlds through the pseudonym tells an understory of still hidden savageries, of our own inexorably expanding prison industry and Stalin's "purges" making Nikolai Bukharin himself a victim in 1938 for his stand against the tyrant's agricultural and industrial collectivizations forcing the Russian people off their lands, out of their homes, and into historical and private vacuums where uncounted millions died and were murdered. How close are we in the hiddenness of this issue so expertly manipulated by our politicians and media to the "pain" haunting the buried historical imagery in this poem, and the visions the poet knows in their "million parts" whispering to us about this "war," the one almost won already selling us into resignation whose price lies outside of any world we know or could belong to without the "transformation" the resigning demands, and with that "invitation" end in a repellant belonging such a whisper can only barely suggest? If authoritarianism is fertilized by distance from an "Other," whatever the hallucinations of the "Other" are, then distance itself as stereotype is even more fertilized by the media. The greater the distance, the greater the punishment and harm.

Perhaps it is easier not to know the terrible historical secrets lying in wait at the end of our prisons' endlessly disinfected corridors. The prisoners themselves know, and it is a secret, rather than giving them superior comfort over their keepers' mindlessness, that makes them even sadder. Most of us don't know prisoners, don't want to. Distance is an easy product to accumulate. The price seems practically non-existent. In confiscating those men and women to the most obscure edges of our moral boundaries, we make it impossible for us to hear their voices, especially those that could tell us about the absolute divestment of morality lying at the threshold of all our futures that will stand for no interference in the formative blueprints of this planned-for, centuries-long industrial complex.

Make no mistake in the wording. The previous centuries of racial distancing have given us the confidence of this century's projection into a future whose violence has been pre-tested in order to perfect what have been up to now imperfect, man-made hells. In a late-twentieth-century world spilling out its deluge of product, each yelling for attention inside a subtle or not so subtle publicity design, the one most silent, malevolent act of production is that of moral indifference. No matter how much this has been said before, it is our perfected product and brings into a harmonious concentration its by-products, prison as the most calculated form of violence against the too-soon-to-be left-over populations, and the rationality that would sweep aside all inhibitions against it.

How good we can get at mining the deterioration of ourselves no one can really know. But there is no doubt that a significant part of our industrial complex wants to be good, fervently good. One of the finest preparations for prison in our culture is the ghetto, no matter what its guise. Its deprivation, orientation, and pain are the twin to incarceration. The experience of racism, its labels of deviance, makes the pain of imprisonment one more wall, one more torture to stare back at. I know men so used to the torture you can throw them into "The Hole" months or even years, and though you'll administer the best industrial pain ever produced or bought, they'll come out, and what you want them to lose they won't. It'll hurt, hurt bad. But it was already lived through so long before that this would be just another rehearsal among a pattern of rehearsals—for sure one that took a bite, and even that bite's a part of a line of rehearsals stretching back to the ghetto and its "pre-incarceration deprivations" that ". . . seem to be 'functional for survival in . . . prison.'" The essay on prison suicide I am quoting from, written by a prisoner with a Master's degree, discusses the fact that those members of society least prepared for the pain and isolation of prison are ". . . predominantly white and middle-class." The body of empirical evidence so far examined indicates that the rates of suicide ". . . among white inmates are disproportionately higher than for either black or Hispanic inmates . . . over a nine year period in the Maryland State prison system white inmates committed suicide at almost twice the rate of black inmates. And in their study of New York State's jail and prison systems, the State Commission of Corrections (1990) found the same 2 to 1 ratio of white to black inmate suicides for the year 1989, and a 4 to 1 ratio of white to Hispanic suicides."

If the historical destinies of our minority, and now possible throwaway populations, are this perfect a fit for prison and the industries of crime control and public safety, then any of our reasons for ignorance, distance, or vengeance become even more a part of the logic of "death principle," as Václav Havel calls it, which we are in the process of embracing. That embrace includes, too, what Senator Daniel Patrick Moynihan said in his 1965 report entitled "The Negro Family: The Case for National Action," about the practice of slavery in America:

> The most perplexing question about American slavery, which has never been altogether explained, and which indeed most Americans hardly know exists, has been stated by Nathan Glazer as follows: "Why was American slavery the most awful the world has ever known?" The only thing that can be said with certainty is that this is true: it was.[18]

In Texas there are choirs who stand outside of prisons while convicts are being given lethal injections and serenade those about to die with "Happy Trails Again." The criteria for vengeance and the unquestioned ease of this totality of contempt pose another divestment, one of the identity for that public whose "safety" demands the invention first and then mass incapacitation of its surplus masses.

When we discuss "public safety," are we talking about the actual historical record of our failure as a people, or are we talking about a public no longer safe from itself, who will look for any means possible to trivialize these more malevolent agencies of its consumption? In addition, are we discussing a public on the verge of being so well-trained by its media and politicians that its training cannot be reversed?

For the first time, we are beginning to spend more on prison than for higher education. The states involved in this emergent fiscal shift are California, Florida, Minnesota, Massachusetts, Connecticut, and Michigan. The corrections authorities in California predict the "peak year" for prison population to be 2027, when there will be at least 401,000 inmates in just this one state system alone, where, since 1980, the monies spent on prisons have risen 500 percent, and the monies for education in the state budget fell 25 percent. The confidence in these numbers indicates how little a limit there is to this growth principle or the sacrifices a "safe" public will not make for it. Whether we listen to the choirs in Texas or drive through the beautiful "hanging valleys" of New York's Finger Lakes region with its array of prisons, de Tocqueville's fear for ourselves as a people in the 1830s may be even more palpable in 1995:

> Democracy leads men not to draw near to their fellow creatures; but democratic revolutions lead them to shun each other and perpetuate in a state of equality the animosities that the state of inequality created.[19]

In this time the picture of a democratically "safe" public holding the yoke of this "equality" carries a chilling burden, for it is the civilly dead million and more prisoners in our human hells now who show us how we are constructing a more debased yoke over ourselves that we may never be able to unbuild, even if we were to begin at this moment. Who holds the yoke in 1997 tells the deeper story of our democracy and the double reflection of its equal/unequal tragedy de Tocqueville fell short of entirely anticipating, not because he couldn't have, but because he didn't want to stomach taking it that far? To paraphrase de Tocqueville, this is where the vices of rulers and the growing ineptitude of the people mix, to become a violating whole: "By this means habits are formed in the heart of a free country which may some day prove fatal . . ."[20]

The reference to the death penalty I began this passage with had an arithmetic of one, as far as my friend was concerned. One man. One death. If the death is a mistake, then the whole coherence of both visible and invisible daily life, the material and the spiritual, loses the indispensable element of its self-awareness and what holds it together, replaced by the shrinkage into comforts that have haunted our utilitarian hungers from the beginning. He was a civilian, like myself on the inside, and did not necessarily like dealing with these men. They were, many of them, murderers, rapists, thieves, contract killers, thugs looking to extort as mean a price on the inside as they did on the outside, because prison is a world, too.

They were also human beings, with families on all sides, victims and predators, paying with humiliation and torment, and themselves condemned to spend a huge portion of their active lives remanded to a nothing. But the state's power had to stop with *their* mistake. To assume an equal and more dangerous mistake of its own initiates a decline of private existence through the increase and display of publicly allowable pain. He became, on this basis, a hostage negotiator with the feeling that all the life he would have to negotiate for, whether the kept or the keeper, was necessary, and in every instance worth saving.

Chapter V
Oblivions

WALK INTO A PRISON and it'll scare you to your core. You get a portrait slowly coming to focus of yourself, that with only the slightest jiggle of what you think are "normal" events you can get your invitation, too. The fear that comes with it can cause you to go two ways. Either you'll ask questions that'll pose no ease anywhere, or you'll ask the questions that'll offer all the "comforts" our utilitarian racism has pushed at us for nearly 500 years. With those "comforts" and their one-way questions, you can begin to refer to your flock, as many of the keepers do, as "porch monkeys" and the solutions in waiting we have for them based on the industrialization of a "public safety." When we examine the NRA's opposition to the ban on the sales and distribution of armor-piercing shells as part of its policy of "public safety," are we, in formulating another painful question, referring to "porch monkeys" and the traditional ordinances that cannot truly harm them? To stop such sub-species, who have no feeling anyway, your cache of normal bullets has up and gone obsolete.

"Arthur" is a Puerto Rican. He is slight, about 5'8", in very good physical condition, and over 50 years old. Among all the Vietnam War veterans I knew in the prisons my program served, Arthur was the most dangerous. Quiet, reserved almost painfully, purposefully invisible, skilled in personal manners, he was a Marine, part of an assassination unit as he identified it, responsible for the destruction of Ngo Dinh Diem and Ngo Dinh Nhu. The "Medusa Battalion," they were called. Stone Killers. Expert in all the forms of soundless murder, the kind where you don't even get the chance to have enough breath for a last sigh. This was his specialty in Vietnam, the recipe he sharpened every day. There were so many bodies he didn't even want to count them. He was also the "boss" behind one of the boldest drug-smuggling incidents to have taken place in our history. The thing perhaps that gave him the most pride after he assumed power on the East Coast for the organization he ran was the total absence of bodies, no corpse trail here at home. He'd shake his head over the contrast and its starkness, how the two opposites could even co-exist. "Not one single body here, Dr. Matlin, not one." Inconspicuous. Arthur would dress in fine suits, carry finer leather brief cases, and ride to business on a bicycle. No limo. No Mercedes. The essentials, whittled down to one directive. He'd done his first 15 years in a Fed, the last ten in New York, and had three more to go before coming up for parole. Twenty-eight years, three spent in solitary confinement. The other source of pride was no tickets. Tickets are infractions the guards write up that'll get you to court, to solitary, sentence extensions, loss of trailer visits, whole horizons of loss inside of loss—not one in 25 years.

The deadliest spider going through all the routine, soft-spoken, precise, disciplined into a fraction of self that measured everything, everybody, directing his money toward an apartment building on Sutton Place for speculation, or a bungalow in the Caribbean. They couldn't break him. They knew it. When his 30 years is up, they have to let him go. Arthur wanted me to ghost-write his story, what he saw, what he knew about the CIA, about experiments Americans have been subjected to that'd turn you inside out. But I don't want to be a ghost. It's what you get to be in prison anyway, and after awhile I began to feel like a part of me had disappeared. I'd look at my hands or feet to see if they were there to see just how much prison had taken, make sure I could rub those parts back into visibility again. The prison where Arthur and 800 others are kept is the slickest the industry has to offer. You go down route 44-55 south of New Paltz, New York, about 17 miles toward the village of Wallkill. The Shawangunk Mountains offer an almost primordial backdrop. The farmlands and valley edging up to the over 400-million-year-old conglomerate cliffs allow the eye to float toward distances and horizons that have no equal to anything I've seen on the East Coast. I'm a Westerner, a native of the Mohave and Sonoran deserts. When my wife, whose heritage is the Hudson Valley going back many generations, pointed out that the Catskills are mountains, it was a fact to her, one I didn't want to fight over, but one that would not easily settle with the comparisons I seem to carry. It would take many years to let go of those comparisons and what they demanded. The western landscapes I come from never really stop their secret whisper inside of me. Their loneliness, hugeness, and silence are my first awakenings. The winds that came moaning out of their valleys to often devastate and haunt the world of my childhood I hear still, the sand and grit they carried scouring the house of my earliest memories, blasting and caving in windows, turning the domestic elegance of my mother's designs into an unrecognizable sinew to be rebuilt at what cost finally to her even in my middle age I can't estimate. I don't know how to say when the Catskills became mountains to me. There was a kind of resistance that had to be shed. The isolated valley where I live is surrounded by their Cambrian ridges. Follow the ravines cutting through the state forests that border our property to their source, and you'll find fossil waterfalls that formed during the glacial melt more than 10,000 years ago. The introductory lures of spring when the stands of weeping willow on the Esopus Creek pop with the burning cold of February bring bald eagles. The great birds are hungry then. Sometimes as many as three or four can be seen perched on hemlock risen above the running, ice-locked waters, heads bent, alert for fish. They'll stay maybe a month, maybe less, the washed out blues of the winter sky holding their shape like no other soaring bird on the way south to the Susquehanna or Mississippi.

On the plateau above us, when temperatures approach 20 below zero, great horned owls gather for nuptial flight. The sexual dance above leaf-stripped hibernating forest in the deepest severity of this winter daylight holds the secret raptures of these hunters whose killing screams we'll hear on the yet-to-appear nights of a distant, and at these moments, almost unimaginable summer. Coyotes'll come down chasing snow-starved deer. The packs howl and circle in the meadows just below our bedroom windows and give us chills that cut to an even more secretive bone than the winter gales moaning down bending the forest with the sound of a specter freight train carrying a cargo of worlds and dreams and galaxies that never has time to make a stop and unload. It's even rumored cougar have returned to the country lying beyond the unvisited remoteness edging the maple-shrouded cliffs, where you can stumble over a sudden 300-foot drop without knowing how you ever arrived to be this flying body of your last unwarned seconds.

I needed this passage through the countryside and wildernesses surrounding the area where I live. The terrible contrasts between it and the prisons I went to helped me to begin to see anew their mystery and the mystery of a humanity, though locked in silence and moral oblivion, that would mark me for life. On the way to the prisons, I'd look out over the Shawangunks. They remind me of mesas, the way they lean on the horizon and the curvature of the earth, with, at certain sunsets, the textures of Venus welling up into the infant darknesses of twilight as I'd peer down into the razor-wired shroud of the world named after these silurian outcrops. The Mohonk Conference was held among these geologic relics from 1883 to 1912 to decide the twentieth-century fates of all the Indians left from the nineteenth-century holocaust. Their reservations in square footage are the largest prisons yet devised.

The old hotel sits on a lake and whole families come still, in the tradition of their grandmothers and grandfathers, for a stay in the civilized wilderness and its pastoral views. You can almost hear the swish of dresses and petticoats, the laughter of long-dead Fifth Avenue gentlemen behind the walls of the great rooms in this hotel. On the huge, shaded veranda where I sat myself one mid-summer evening, a woman in her late 80s was escorted by her great-grandsons. This excursion had taken place for at least 60 years to verify that here at least the images from her childhood had suffered no change.

Prison. The town I started my life in California was a prison town. I didn't remember that either until I got this job. It was an experimental facility for "model prisoners." The convicts had jobs outside but had to be back by the end of a working day. There was a fence, yet any man could escape. If he did that, then he was no longer fit to be a model anything. It was an honor system, an honor to do time there. A movie was made about this prison. The movie director went on to a career in both film and TV. His wife, whom he met on location, taught Spanish in the local high school to my older brother and his friends and was the sister of a famous Los Angeles painter. Prison swelling its spinnerets. The women's jail was down the road in a nearby town. It was a main holding pen for all the female criminals in California at the time I was a kid. I can remember riding by at night in the back seat of my parents' car going over the faces I'd seen on *Dragnet* stopping at the occasional woman, wondering what window held her stare. My mother's voice came to a halt before this prison and would not start easily again until we'd gotten almost home. The repugnant glare of those night-time windows that struck my mother dumb over 40 years ago in the then-rural California countryside were evidence, I was later to come to learn, of her private convictions about being a woman, about being marginal, being part-Indian, being invisible. Jail in the full condition of its dismissal of the already-even-born-to-be-dismissed, was an image that invaded her.

Some of the people I know in prison will escape anytime they get the chance. One man, in for murder, got out in the mid-70s. He slowly built a guard toward a final bribery and then walked from a maximum-security warehouse as if it were somebody else's hallucination he didn't need to be in one more second, got in a waiting car, and sped away, living for eight years on borrowed time until he was put in chains in San Francisco and shipped back. He made an ass out of the whole system with that escape. Ever since, he's been on special watch, a legend among both convicts and keepers, no one knowing when he might conjure his powers for another attempt; he's so good the authorities have to be on permanent red alert even though they've got him in the most controlled hell your money can buy.

Another man has been given sixty-seven years. He's done seventeen, with fifty more to go. Three escapes. More to come if he gets the chance. Guaranteed. In for an execution. "They should have pinned a medal on me, Doc, for icing that scum. I did the whole world a favor." Then he'd write beautiful analyses of Guy Davenport or Julio Cortázar. Along with a couple of others, he had the most finely tuned Marxist and liberation-theology critiques I've ever heard. Colombian drug runners and scholars.

In the fall of 1994, the last semester I taught in the program, four men escaped. The local neighborhoods were so frightened they let gangs of corrections officers search their homes from top to bottom. The thought of those demons running loose almost loosened the rural population surrounding Shawangunk from its mental pins. Who knows where those beasts could have been hidden? They would have done better to just stare through their iron-barred windows. By the time they got through the webs of steel and the electric barrier, they were half-butchered by razor wire, cut to the marrow from head to toe, and wandering in a blood-loss delirium. All were captured within a couple of days, the last as close to the border between living and dying as you can get with your last pints oozing out.

Another way to escape is to just get stabbed in the heart. That's what happened to another "student." One day in the yard somebody tried to do some surgery on his aorta. He got a helicopter escort out of Naponoch straight to Albany Med where it took hours to put back the shred into its previous resemblance of a pump. No one'll say who the assailant was. The reasons for the attack could stem from snitching, a lovers' quarrel, making good on a threat, a personal insult; you can throw your guesses into a pit till sundown.

The eruptions of frustration, self-hatred, contempt, and extortion are the abysmal trenches lying below the surface of this sea. Even in the areas designated for education, these negations and their impulses could spill. If a fight broke out in my classes, either verbally or physically, and fights did, I stopped them. In one literature course, there was a Vietnam veteran, jittery, very ill. Another prisoner baited him one night, belittled his combat experience. I jumped in the middle of whatever was going to get started, a very stupid act on my part. I could have yelled for guards. I could have. But all the years of trust that had been constructed would have disintegrated instantly. The men would have been key-locked, even put in the "Hole." If you couldn't take this business, you had no business being there.

Incidents beyond the classroom could also occur. An almost-riot started. Two men from nowhere locked in a whirl of fists and kicking feet, then two more, multiplying in the ways these numbers just step into a space, then grab pencils and stab anything that comes in range. The prisoner with the barely pumping heart got to experience a kind of miracle. He "died" in one prison, Naponoch, and when he completely woke up months later, he was in another, Shawangunk. The power of resurrection, even reincarnation, works in mysterious ways in prison. He looked at me one late afternoon on a sweltering summer day, said if he told who did the "shank" work on him, he'd never see the light of a next morning.

Chapter VI
Venus and Mars

GHOSTS TALK IN PRISON. The fear shrouding their words is germinal, reaching back to shadows when life slurped at the trickles of its own lifelessness and form fused with the symptoms of its unbearable abhorrence to come into the destitution of any "likeness" or "being."

Chapter VII
Point Blank

THE ENTRANCE ROAD to Shawangunk cuts through some of the most spectacular farm country in the Hudson Valley, or maybe anywhere. It's the best-groomed concrete in New York State. Street lamps spaced at about 50 yards on both sides line this passage. You think it's a mistake at first. No other public roadway provides this sort of immaculate insulation against common or unexpected driving hazards. It is as well-lit as any California freeway for about two felicitous miles. Then it's over. A normal drive in the New York State countryside demands a "clear physical eye" as opposed to "the erring brain," to quote the poet Louis Zukofsky. The "erring brain" can drive you directly into deer, which can maim and kill as efficiently as an oak, the bear that I've personally crashed into, and concrete that almost invites car wrecks it's so badly kept and maintained. Turn off 44-55 toward this prison, and another illumination smoulders. There are two waiting on the downside of this grade. Wallkill to the left is a "medium." Built in the late 40s and early 50s, it's a short-time pen for most, those who've got walking papers but will have to wait six months or five years or ten before they're released, and some quiet ones who'll do life in this supposedly easier camp. There are shipments in chains, all the time. Guys are learning optics, electricity, cookery, baking, farm labor, welding, pure-bred horse grooming, general maintenance. There is also a dairy to supply all the local "clientele" with milk, and don't mess with the cows who are "family" to the milkers, who know each animal by name, sound, tail swish. A pond fronts this "facility," and every fall flocks of Canadian geese circle, land, and fill the frosting night air with their pre-migrational honking, gossiping. The sky becomes an air show then. The sunsets hold these circling, waiting birds by the thousands, landing gear flexed against the blaze of dying sun and the heatless days settled in the roar of their cumulative chatter. You can almost imagine a mastodon coming for a late-afternoon sip, as they did once, too, before these cliffs, a calf panicking the geese for fun, hundreds of powerful wings snapped to minimal unison and churning water in a mass frustration.

Shawangunk is a "maxi-max." It's down further at the end on the right. Don't take a casual drive unless you've got a reason and can explain it. Binocular-wielding guards are ready to take your license-plate numbers, the make of your car, the color. It looks like the last version of a butcher block; thinned, whittled, that alphabetical "P" in front of the word "prison" dripping with cancellation. I remember a number of years ago, when I lived in New York City, walking by the Tombs one day. It seemed all the hookers north of Fourteenth Street had been let out to cuss, hustle, primp, pose, then fan out toward Chinatown and Little Italy, some throwing mirrors that showed unappreciated images and used-up lipstick tubes into the neighborhood gutters, laughing, stomping high heels, sharing smokes of name-brand tobacco, or maryjane.

The Tombs was shut down not long after that. A renovation had begun. I knew a young woman from Bennington College who was seeing an architect, and her first date was a tour. He was working for the firm contracted to redesign that jail and wanted to show her the work in progress. These two children of the upper class walked through the hell they were designing for the lower.

It's hard to bring up that word "class." I've been trying to avoid it. But the conjunction of architecture and punishment makes such avoidance into yet one more emasculation and debasement. The act of "tourism" and its assumptions that took place in the Tombs that day in the 1970s, the regalia of blueprints shown, are an intersection of services, practices, and reductions that have become so masked in the naturalism of allowable threat that we have no way of naming their mutilations. Noam Chomsky in *The Prosperous Few and the Restless Many* points out how not only are we not allowed to discuss class differences in the United States, but these censorships and the impoverishing illusions that fuel them have made it "impossible to talk." There are fewer and fewer pieces of vocabulary that can tell us about suffering. "Tourism." The dictionary says this word means "the practice of traveling for recreation." Often while traveling to work through countryside filled with bear and coyote, I'd picture that couple in the Tombs—the proud young architect standing in the midst of the concentration of power he was designing; the young woman, his "date," examining new cell blocks, wash basins, concrete reinforcement that would fix and code bodies into the monotony of preventative space. I'd also hear that dictionary definition, its whisper tightening in my throat. I couldn't help but think about my own privilege and "class"; that I might be a secret tourist, too. Every time I drove toward this razorwired science of penalty, I'd have to raise a dam in my mind over questions. Often, no matter how well constructed I felt that dam was, it disintegrated, the windshield of my car filling with the flood of this facility's profile and the "attentive malevolence," transforming all that it touches into myself, Michel Foucault says in *Discipline & Punish: The Birth of the Prison*, was born "... at the threshold of the contemporary period . . ." in the seventeenth century.

The magazine *Corrections Today* can provide a helpful hint. The marriage of architecture and "justice" fills its pages. "Sprung Instant Structures," for instance, can meet an order for a 400 inmate-capacity prison in 25 days. Tindell Concrete Products, Inc. introduced an advertisement in the June, 1995, issue with the following lead: "The State of Florida is determined to keep criminals locked up for at least 75 percent of their sentences by December 1995. An acute bed shortage must not get in the way . . . Tindell Concrete is part of the answer. Using fully equipped and furnished fairi cell modules, factory cast of high-strength reinforced concrete, Florida will meet its deadline." Kitchell CEM (Capital Expenditure Management) boasts, "Over the past 15 years, we've managed the planning, design and construction of 100,000 beds. That's more than $5 billion in projects. And today, we are the leading firm in the business . . ." The Dick Group of Companies in Pittsburgh state that its group ". . . has grown to become one of the nation's leading builders of correctional facilities . . ." They have completed, or have under construction, 19 projects, comprising 24,500 beds with a construction cost of more than $1 billion. "HLM Justice" ". . . in the last ten years . . . has designed over 10 million square feet of cost-effective, efficiently-planned justice facilities . . ." all across the United States. This firm of architects, engineers, and planners has key locations in Charlotte, Chicago, Denver, Philadelphia, Iowa City, Portland Oregon, New York, Orlando, Sacramento, and Washington, D.C. CRSS Constructors, Inc. are "Corrections project delivery specialists" who have "45 corrections projects / programs exceeding $3.2 billion since 1986 . . ." across twelve states.

"CRSS," in identifying itself as a "delivery specialist," uses the language of the Cold War. Every nuclear-bomb contractor was and is a "delivery specialist," and these numbers in their boastful billions are Cold War numbers. Silver & Ziskind, architects, planners, interior designers, have a Park Avenue address. This international firm offering ". . . fast track design . . ." has set ". . . new standards in correctional architecture for the past two decades. Providing award winning, innovative, cost effective and context-sensitive designs for a growing and changing industry."

The "context sensitive" terminology employed here can be translated through a description of what "context" is. In an article in *Corrections Today* entitled "Design Meets Mission at New Federal Max Facility," there is a description of the Administrative Maximum Facility, or ADX, in Florence, Colorado. This site has been designed to "consolidate" offenders into one "super max" camp who are considered to be disruptive, predatory, extremely violent, escape-prone. The most heavily secured section of the 562-bed ADX in Florence is called the "Control Unit." It has 68 beds and contains what are called the ". . . most dangerous and assaultive inmates . . ." in the BOP (Federal Bureau of Prisons). In order to be condemned to this form of confinement, prisoners must undergo a "due process hearing." If all elements of qualification are met, the prisoner then spends 23 hours per day in a 90-square-foot cell, eats in the cell, "recreates" alone seven hours per week. If an inmate "demonstrates good conduct" in the ADX, he can descend from the "Control Unit" to five under-units containing lessened degrees of detention. The ADX has more than 1,400 electronically controlled doors, and over 160 cameras to monitor every corridor grill and door critical to security. "In addition to main and inside control centers from which officers can monitor all corridors and electronically control all corridor grills, each unit has its own control center from which the officer can monitor all ranges and electronically control all cell doors." The individual cell has plumbing fixtures that are "flood proof." Built-in, tamper-proof, electric cigarette lighter, a sink, a toilet, a shower "... so inmate privacy is increased and inmate movement is decreased." Push buttons are also a feature to "... reduce the amount of moving parts." To this point such description sounds like the most cost-heavy not-in-orbit space station ever devised. Why go extraterrestrial "out there" when you can just as easily undergo the manual of deprivations training directly under the shadows of the Rocky Mountains? "Context sensitive" requirements also apply to inmate restraint policies:

> Control unit inmates, for example, are cuffed and leg shackled before they leave their cell. Three officers escort each control unit inmate. General population unit inmates are cuffed from behind for all movement and require a two-person escort ... ADX staff consider gang affiliation, past history, and racial and ethnic factors before assigning inmates to cells and units. Intelligence gathering by all staff is critical to spot potential inmate conflicts.[21]

Taxonomy and punishment interweave here to form multiple effects and to insure that those effects receive as much distribution as possible throughout the five chains of hierarchy beginning with "Control," and moving, through the demonstration of "good conduct," to "Special Housing Unit," "General Population Units," "Intermediate Unit,"

"Transitional Unit," and "Pretransfer Unit." The surveillance of every whisper, defecation, bodily twitch in sleep can be more rigorously mapped, assessed so that these "difficult-to-manage inmates" will re-emerge as products bearing a lessened threat to the smooth operation of other prisons that will receive and lock them down, as well as to the safety of staff, other prisoners, and "the public." The "public" that can be threatened by a man with a three-officer escort—cuffed, leg shackled, walking as if each step will pull out the bones in his wrists, ankles, and legs—is a "public" that has transformed this man into one of its most vital commodities. An architectural firm not "context sensitive" to this commodity and its uses will not survive if it desires to compete in this industry.

The affirmation of prison as cultural and historical monument can be further found in a recent exhibition (August, 1995) in Philadelphia. Eastern State Penitentiary opened for business in 1829 and closed in 1971—142 years of life for one site. The British architect John Haviland designed this prison. His blueprint has been the foundation for more than 300 prison constructions internationally and domestically. At the time of its construction, this building was the most costly in America, the first to have indoor plumbing, the first with 12-foot-thick 30-foot-high granite containment walls. It was a preview ADX. The rule was iron silence here, solitary confinement for each convict in an 8-by-12 foot cell. Madness broke out in the 1830s. A visitor, Charles Dickens, was so repelled by what he saw in 1842 he wrote:

> I hold this slow and daily tampering with the mysteries of the brain, to be immeasurably worse than any torture of the body: and because its ghastly signs and tokens are not so palpable to the eye and sense

of touch as scars upon the flesh; because its wounds are not upon the surface, and it extorts few cries that human ears can hear; therefore I the more denounce it, as a secret punishment which slumbering humanity is not roused up to stay.[22]

Dickens, in his words after witnessing the "buried alive" and his own personal despair before it, admitted in a letter to David C. Colden in March, 1842, "... I never in my life was more affected by anything which was not strictly my own grief, than I was by this sight. It will live in my recollection always." John Haviland's prison is a national landmark, and the art exhibition entitled "Prison Sentences" is an attempt to preserve his "monument." There is a too-cozy alignment here between the industries of the arts and prison. The promotion of name recognition for the artists and their site-specific works for this so-called "gallery space" is at the forefront of emphasis. A *New York Times* review in the summer of 1995 of this "show" stated, "Perhaps the show's best known artist, Jonathan Borofsky, has contributed a flying figure—representing a ghost shadow of prisoners past—and chalked inscriptions on a cell wall. The inscriptions set down what might be convicts' recollections of their dreams. One reads, 'falling back to sleep again, I envisioned the top part of my mind removed.' It is accompanied by a sketch of a human head with a piece missing." The men I knew were capable of far more work in dream and language than these stilted, deadened terms proposed by Mr. Borofsky.

Another artist "... uses slabs of fallen plaster from the decaying prison to seal one cell's doorway. In a second cell, he piles a mound of powdered plaster in the form of a crater, seemingly offering no escape. In a third, there is another mound of powder spreading over the bottom of a metal prison bed, perhaps providing an exit route. The piece also contains a labyrinth. 'That's a Hopi Indian labyrinth signifying emergence into another world' the artist explains. 'My piece has to do with the origin of a sense of penitence—rather than punishment.'" How this artist arrived at once at such a use of "Hopi" material, debased intellectual foreground, and his own "paradox" of indifference may be answered by Marc Mauer's warning that the continued usage of prisons makes their presence not just "logical and rational," but in the case of the men and women in this "exhibition," a normal extension of personal career in which prison, in spite of the positive intents of individual artists, wraps them also in the "context-sensitive" shadows of the industry of crime control and its veneration and worship.

Hansen Lind Meyer, Inc., or "HLM Justice" out of Iowa City, has offices "nationwide" and a staff of at least 300 architects, planners, engineers, and construction managers. Its 10 million square feet of "justice facilities" in the United States and abroad amount to $5 billion. CRSS Constructors, Inc., the Dick Group of Companies, "HLM Justice," and Kitchell CEM represent $14.2 billion worth of business. "Justice facility" has an almost holy sound to it, a resonant point of purity placing any would-be questions about its legitimacy into the same realm of illegitimacies as that which it hides and confines. Nils Christie, to whose essay "Crime Control As Industry" I referred earlier, demonstrates how our media and politicians have intermixed crime and sin, inventing a ground of preparation where a sacred war without limit is in the process of appearing in which prison "... may be seen as the most essential of all needs." Dr. Christie states how and why this industry is here, how and why its potential capacity has come to be in place. The upper two-thirds of our population in the United

States, he explains, have a standard of living far richer "for so large a proportion of a nation" than any other in the world and a mass media that flourishes "... on reports on the dangers of the crimes committed by the remaining one-third of the population. Rulers are elected on promises to keep the dangerous third behind bars...."[23] He at once asks why these trends should stop and states that there are no natural limits for the rational minds who would mine the one-third as mineral wealth in a "New Jack" economy. The forces of morality and basic values have their most solid conjunctions here. Why should the interests behind these forces not succeed completely?

> Germany was able to do it, to reach a final solution in the middle
> of a war, despite the urgent need to make alternative use of its railways
> as well as of the guards. The USSR was able to develop the Gulags
> in the midst of preparations for war, and to run them during and
> after it. They were not only able to do so, but benefited from the
> arrangements. Why should not modern, industrialized nations be
> even more successful? [24]

Dr. Christie reminds us how the tasks of internment and genocide were close to impossible for these two societies and, in turn, given the proper set of tactics, how much easier it would be for us to "manage" the new dangers the lower one-third presents to the upper two-thirds:

> The ground has been prepared. The media prepare it every day and
> night. Politicians join ranks with the media. It is impossible politi-
> cally not to be against sin. This is a competition won by the highest
> bidder. To protect people from crime is a cause more just than any.
> At the same time, the producers of control are eagerly pushing for

orders. They have the capacity. There are no natural limits. A crime-free society is such a sacred goal for so many, that even money does not count. Who asks about costs in the middle of a total war?[25]

If one were to examine the symptoms of this "total war" and its ground of profit, *Corrections Today* would be a place to begin. It is the showcase of industry hardware, supply, and technological invention. In the pages of this slicksheet, you can find everything from "The Violent Prisoner Chair" produced by AEDEC International to Point Blank Body Armor in Amityville, New York. Point Blank's ad in the August, 1995, issue states, "Some inmates would *love* to stab, slash, pound, punch, and burn you. But they won't get past your S.T.A.R. or Special Tactical Anti-Riot Vest with slash protection achieved with space-age titanium blunt trauma protection." This ad further informs the potential buyer that "... you'll barely feel the blows ..." The S.T.A.R. vest also protects the wearer from potential fire hazards with a fire retardant "Nomex" covering and exhorts the reader at the end of the copy with a final pun of "... Don't get stuck with anything less ..." A customer can order "Clincher Wristbands"; security-transfer vehicles from "Blue Bird Security" featuring five types of vehicles with "inmate capacity from 12 to 60"; "Nicholson's Liquid Beverage Bases," "... all vitamin-C enriched ..." from the H.R. Nicholson Company in Baltimore; "Padded Surfaces by B & E"; "Home Detention Technology" designed by Mitsubishi and Ameritech, which features video-display telephones to identify "... client at home ..."; a breath-alcohol tester that "... automatically transmits a picture of the client with test results to the host computer ..." and speaker I.D. Goya Foods displays its name in full-page pictures.

Corrections Today demonstrates how simplified the model of supply and management has become, the logic of "war" profit and its promise of an as yet unimpeded future, and an already staggering dependence of our culture on the "industry." Newt Gingrich, in a speech in Cleveland in July, 1995, offered a much more precise sense of promise, election, and the sacredness related to this "war." His presentation on the steps to his version of national recovery included both incarceration and punishment. But Mr. Gingrich's focus on illegal drug sales, importation, and children can tell us more about a "holy" crime crusade than almost any other political rhetoric so far given: "We love our children so much we'll kill you," he warned all potential mules and smugglers. The will to hatred and panic soaking this rhetoric tells us how close we are to the exercise of a terrible diminishment; in Nils Christie's words, "There are no particular reasons for optimism. There is no easy way out, no prescription for a future where the worst will not come to the worst . . ."[26]

Chapter VIII
Extracts

THE PICTURES OF HELICOPTERS hovering above the U.S. Embassy in Saigon in 1975 included news shots of American soldiers handing children, old women, and luggage to the desperate flight crews. Arms, hands, torsos outstretched in the panic and hysteria the photographs still hold. "William" was one of the soldiers on that roof. When I met him in 1987, he had the faraway glare of other Vietnam veterans. Maybe the horizon he saw from that precipice didn't even have letters to spell a name with. The collapse he directly experienced had to do with passes, whether the people of Saigon bending the gates of the American compound had passes, whether he'd let them in, let them see the calendar he saw of an American fate he would come to know and his place personally in it sliced into undigestible chunks by the Huey rotors. I don't know how finally being the receiver of such an instance of historical squalor, fraud, and final evasion William was wrenched. He had given it an assessment, one that cut through some of the degradation, just for his own sanity. He wrote about and discussed it, but how far he or anyone else could drive that assessment toward the stinking shadows of treacheries that engulf it, I don't really know. I do know William was down for drugs. The authorities wanted him so bad they attempted to bring down his whole family: grandmother, grandfather, father, mother, siblings. Held them in the Federal Detention Center in Lower Manhattan to get to the son.

He'd signed up for a composition course for a break from his "normal" prison job. William could tell stories, too, bend them into funny-sad parts, put them back together, not lose one knot of the narration, one invisible brace. I noticed that his face and ears were a perpetual red, though, eyes smoked with fear. I didn't understand at first. He'd barely talk, but would do his assignments right enough, every time in writing. William was one of the only orderlies for AIDS patients in the prison that confined him and the suffering men he watched over. He was the one to hear last whispers, let those drifting so brutally away in a prison know they were still human to somebody. He was a Vietnam War veteran in prison watching over dying junkies and homosexuals also in prison who'd got the plague. What more alien, dangerous, and septic combination could there possibly have been in that year of 1987 to the forces of misinformation, massive public indifference, and official lack of action?

He wrote an essay about the hospital section in that prison where he administered what little help he could. Cold panic and sweat soaked his prison greens every day. AIDS. William saw it, how it reduced its host, inflamed, disfigured what was supposed to be a human body. That essay nearly made me panic. His panic, was over whether he'd got too close, whether one of those dying whispers had somehow seeped in, passed through the veil of flesh without his knowing and started its work. From that roof in Saigon to an AIDS infirmary in a New York State maximum-security prison, he was too close each time and Luck draining from the c or the k with no plug anywhere. My near panic was over my son. His essay did that. I knew people or heard of acquaintances, then, who'd been diagnosed with HIV but had seen none of the deeper wounding that infection brought. The epidemic first appeared in the U.S. in 1981. The first public recognition on Ronald Reagan's part took place on May 31, 1987. Six years and 36,058 Americans were diagnosed with the symptoms, and over 20,000 were dead from its effects: the word *Indifference* again and its force mixed with the images of deviants and persons with the wrong color from the wrong populations.

The Reverend Jerry Falwell claimed, "AIDS is God's judgment of a society that does not live by his rule," and Senator Jesse Helms stated, "The logical outcome of testing is a quarantine of those infected."[27] The perfect disease for official lack of action, for the elimination of the unwanted. William was Jewish. He had volunteered for the orderly job in an obscure, badly equipped penitentiary hospital, and had seen the mental and physiological collapse of the victims. He wrote about the crisis of AIDS in prisons, how much finally he thought it might cost. He'd gone almost numb from it, was on the edges of nervous breakdown. We had friends at that time, a couple with one son who'd gone to a fine private college, graduated, and was coming toward the beginnings of a full adulthood when he collapsed on a sidewalk in New York City, was taken to a hospital, and died there from the symptoms of AIDS at the age of 30. No one knows whether his encounter was with a female or male; it doesn't matter. That young man and the sidewalk that caught his body have haunted me ever since. What do I tell my son, also our only child, and how in such a telling do I not so frighten and fill him with shame that he ends up poisoned over this most necessary, humane, and fulfilling human act?

We have close friends now who are dying of this disease. One, very dear to our family, is brave, deeply unselfish, and has led a life of charmed journeys. He's known our son almost since his first breath. On my fiftieth birthday, my wife and son gave a surprise party, and my friend was among a number of others who generously came their personal distances. I had not seen him in maybe a year, a year and a half. He was thin, more than usual, in pain, had sores on his face and hands that I could see even from the lawn I crossed to greet him. During the party we were able to talk, and he told me what I feared most to already know, that he had the full-blown symptoms of AIDS; he said, "There's no reversal from this one." He looked at my eyes wandering toward his hands said again, "Kaposi's sarcoma." The breakages mostly had taken place in his feet and legs, but the evidences of the pustules were obvious on the rest of his body. My friend was also capable of taking wonderful and sometimes not necessarily easy chances. A long time ago he took a chance on me and published my first book. The rock-bruised farm he came from on the Connecticut coast often offered little solace for this homosexual man, but it gave him a cast of unusual courage to overcome what could have been crippling injuries that wait around the secret corners of every farm, and the tortured shame of being a homosexual in a world filled with homophobic poison. He has also been my son's close friend for all his life, so when the party was over and all those people who have meant so much to my life had walked out our door to go their way again, my son came to me and asked not what was wrong, but, "Is that AIDS?" He wasn't so much scared as sad. Our son was then 17 years old. There is nothing we can or want to do about his curiosities or his urges. He has to be a human being. We do talk to him, however, about the mistakes he can make, that some will carry their prices of memory, even regret, maybe shame, but that those, too, will offer him an exploration of what at last will make him who he will be. The one simple mistake that can haunt his life with this kind of death is the one we also talk about, not every day. Yet we talk about precautions, desire, thinking especially when thinking is that last thing any of us want to do. We can't lock our kid away from the world, don't want to, and wish fervently some of the conversation gets heard. He wrote our friend, saying, "I wish I could say 'get better,' but since I can't say that, I'll just say 'get well as you can.'" My friend responded to my son, in return,

> I wish you *had* said that you would like to say "get well." It's not only a problem of my being superstitious, but I'm beginning to discover that our cells have an intelligence and sometimes an independence— such that they can place demands on our willingness to control and compete, especially the result of powers of suggestibility, whether from my own misguided input or the suggestibility of associates and surrogates. You can see how someone in my condition can fall into a philosophic mode, but always attempting various angles.

My son's friend and mine is now dead. He wrote such passages often, and for my son there is no fright; that has been replaced by sadness and quiet laughter over this man's shy humor, love, and bravery before what happened to him.

Of the 64,952 prisoners incarcerated in the New York State prison system in 1995, approximately 12 percent or 7,794 were HIV-positive. The total number of prisoners to have contracted the disease at that point was 2,697. Of those, 1,749 had died. In terms of mortality rates for all inmate deaths in the New York State prison system, the numbers available for the years 1986-91 indicate that two-thirds of the total mortality rate was due to AIDS. AIDS-related illnesses accounted for 65.6 percent of all inmate deaths between 1986 and 1991. For female prisoners, the numbers were much higher. Eighty-eight percent of all female prisoner deaths in New York State were attributable to AIDS. In 1988, 17 percent of New York State's prisoners were HIV-positive. In 1990 15 percent, in 1992 with the last numbers 12 percent. Since Ronald Reagan's first statement about AIDS in 1987, the total number of AIDS cases to have been recorded is 548,102. The total number of deaths is 343,000. The estimated number of Americans with HIV is 650,000 to 900,000.

I can remember during that period seeing things that I wasn't supposed to see, long prison corridors lying emptied except for pools of blood marking one section of that space from another, pools representing shank work that had been performed. Guards of lower rank stationed themselves at what they thought were safe distances while a commanding officer stood over the swollen puddles, face cracked with horror over this part of the job and the threat swimming in those little oceans he didn't want to go near. No bodies. Just this leakage. Clientele with their seas inside of them ready now truly to infect, bring the officers within this unsteady reach, touch wives and children in a closure no penitentiary wall, no matter how thick or high, would ever hold. You could see in his face, even if he had a thumb as big as the cliffs overlooking the prison where he stood, it wouldn't necessarily hold back this dam, especially when the subjugated liquids didn't have to be any bigger or smaller than a drop, the one that got away and jumped from where it was supposed to be contained into his eyes somehow, or nostril and lip edges that weren't covered. When night arrived and I'd walk past the electric gates into the depths of those prisons where the classrooms were located, some of the guards had taken to wearing masks and clear surgical gloves— they didn't want to be breathed on, touched—or I'd see a man in chains being processed by those officers, who acted like they'd taken a direct tube from the Center for Disease Control, a black or Hispanic man locked from his neck to his toes surrounded by the disgusted keepers, terrified over the small precautions a molecule from the kept could slip through. Prisoners on the way to the yard and programs stopped at central points and were searched by officers who hated to touch, hated the proximity demanded of them while their commanders stood watching. William was afraid. He'd gotten off the roof of the American Embassy alive. That was one miracle. Now he was here, but he wouldn't abandon the men he knew who were dying; he would stay to help them into their deaths, then request different work. He became for the other prisoners an object of quiet, firm respect, a man who asked nothing, was studying, struggling toward a college degree in a warehouse, and the masked, gloved guards were unable to fix or immobilize a "punishment" ready equally to extort and condemn them.

What I saw brings to life Michel Foucault's great study *Discipline & Punish: The Birth of the Prison*. During the nearly ten years of my experience, I could not bring myself to read this book in spite of being directed toward it by two close friends. Perhaps if I had read Foucault, my anger against prisons might have prevented me from ever going to the job I had. I don't really know. I might have just thought, too, it was more theory completely disconnected from the actual prisons and real prisoners I knew; but his care, clarity, and the preoccupations that inform them provide recognition before dissimulation, compassion before exclusion.

Foucault traces the appearance of plague and the evolution of the ". . . coercion over bodies, gestures, and behavior . . ."[28] from its eighteenth-century beginnings to our present. The seams of mass infection and the implementation of authoritarian suppression were fundamentally embraced to become a new body of disciplines, transmission, and accounting systems whose consequences and morbidities are at the stale core our "New Jack" economy is in, both as to its certainties and the representation of the spoiled future that will rise up to extract its frozen spaces and killing surveillances, to paraphrase Foucault, from whoever we are about to become in that future. "Everyone locked up in his cage, everyone at his window, answering to his name and showing himself when asked—it is the great review of the living and the dead." Foucault tells us of the mass lockdowns that took place, and the deaths, abnormal behavior, and symptoms which were observed, recorded, and turned into documents of absolute control:

> The registration of the pathological must be constantly centralized. The relation of each individual to his disease passes through the representatives of power, the registration they make of it, the decisions they take on it.[29]

When a man like Jesse Helms uses the word "quarantine," then he is calling upon, whether he knows it or not, the darkest of forced entries, seizures, and strangulations of privacy that have their sources in the attempts to regulate, before the mysteries of the plague, the ". . . smallest details of everyday life . . ." The plague animated new orders of discipline, confinement, and sentences of death:

The plague-stricken town, traversed throughout with hierarchy, surveillance, observation ... the town immobilized by the functioning
of an extensive power that bears in a distinct way over all individual
bodies—this is the utopia of the perfectly governed city ... In order
to see perfect disciplines functioning, rulers dreamt of the state of
plague ...[30]

If this is the "utopia" a Jerry Falwell or a Jess Helms imagines, with
prison and AIDS as the defining central elements of regulation and
separation, then we are standing inside that moment where we chance
upon a deadness and where nothing after the deadness's introduction
will be left to chance, imagination, or the life we thought we had but
instead hung out to dry on the "Trees of Malice" and the sum of their
permeation. We are at the threshold of a plague for which there is no
cure. Come down with HIV and you're dead. The two ugliest tragedies
at work here are, first, the almost perfect historical fit between plague
as it has been defined since the seventeenth century and the automatic
function and mechanisms of "correction" that lead to new, more refined
definitions of crime control, prison, separation, and normal versus
abnormal. The second tragedy is that identified by the great Cuban
novelist Reinaldo Arenas, who was able to write in his memoir *Before
Night Falls* when he was dying of AIDS:

I do not know what it is. Nobody really knows. I have spoken with
dozens of doctors and it is a puzzle to all of them. Illnesses related
to AIDS are treated, but the actual nature of AIDS seems to be a state
secret. I can attest, though, that as a disease it is different from all
others. Diseases are natural phenomena, and everything natural is
imperfect and can somehow be fought and overcome. But AIDS is

a perfect illness because it is so alien to human nature and has as its function to destroy life in the most cruel and systematic way. Never before has such a formidable calamity affected mankind. Such diabolic perfection makes one ponder the possibility that human beings may have had a hand in its creation.

Moreover, all the rulers of the world, that reactionary class always in power, and the powerful within any system, must feel grateful to AIDS because a good part of the marginal population, whose only aspiration is to live and who therefore oppose all dogma and political hypocrisy, will be wiped out.[31]

The disease, in its second decade, has become all too "normal" and, in that, as others have pointed out, with the onset of its normalization a new indifference has set in with a twin force of acceptable permanence.

Chapter IX
The Call

"CHARLES" WAS A PIMP. He began his studies in remedial reading and writing. He'd started at this time a dietary and weight-lifting regime. Lifting weights was normal for many guys. Everyone does "time" his own way. Nearly every night in those "classrooms," you could hear two things out the windows: basketballs slapped into yard concrete, the equal impact of running feet, backboard slams; and barbells being set, the insulated crush of steel packed evenly on each side of the bar, followed by the reps, hours of it. Charles was barely able to read or write, but he wanted his college education, and a "perfect" body. Both were directed by diet and unremitting discipline. To bring his prison menu into line with the selective formula demanded by body-building was an act of imagination in itself. To get the vegetable and protein formulas from the outside was a near impossibility, which he managed, in part, to overcome. Since Charles had to send for his special formulas through the mail, and since those formulas in their powdered form looked like other substances, he had to wait for the elaborate gate inspections for clearance. Prison is a world and with designated monies, extortion, bribes, and sex, you can get almost anything, from women to drugs to fine foods. Inside/outside. The barrier doesn't matter; its razor-wired veil is full of leaks. I remember the appearance of cocaine, once, when some of the students were caught in the college section, put in solitary confinement, indeterminate sentences pushed into a further abyss of time, which probably was worth the lines they'd been able to get. "Corrections" didn't work that day. College and reality met in a little embrace.

Charles came to terms with the English language, mastered all the exercises of reading and writing the program demanded, wrote thoughtful, strong essays equal to those of any advanced student on the outside. He also composed one of the coldest appraisals I've ever seen. It was about "players," what they know about women, about the game they hold and the "book" of rules that informs it:

> The book is so large and deep that it covers every avenue of the game. There are no bitches immune to the jewels contained in the book; each and every one is a potential target . . . In the wrong hands the book could prove fatal to an aspiring player; or in unknowing hands it could prove basically useless . . . The unwritten book contains a wide range of information that exposes the hidden psychological, philosophical, and emotional weaknesses of the true bitch. What's the true bitch? The true bitch is one that tends to be in a constant state of suggestibility . . . For a girl who isn't in a heightened state of suggestibility the player must use a game of mental dress with her, sending out his army to destroy, weaken, and break down the forces that protect her . . . If successful, she's in checkmate and the player is on the road to riches. If not successful then desperation takes over. I hate to mention the fact, but drugs play a major role in making the

good bitch dependent . . . I don't like their aspect of this part of the book, but rules are rules. I didn't make them.[32]

His body also went through a transformation. He became a body-building-contest participant and winner, had articles written about him, corresponded with persons on the outside, and met the woman who would become his future bride while he was still locked up. He was an important example to the men in college and the men grappling with their various decisions to take the qualifying tests, and begin their personal climbs. When I last saw him, he was in civilian clothes, bags packed at the gate, about to go out on parole to a new marriage and life, a little scared but truly happy. A couple of years later, I heard Charles got violent somewhere and was back on the inside for committing a messy ugly murder, never to go out again. That was a fear everyone had who valued the program. The one or two men who'd get the surety of public recognition, get out and do some really vicious crime, and because of that have the media and politicians scream over the college degrees that had been "given" to such criminals, ignoring all the others who had found a life and way out never to return to any prison anywhere.

The corridors of one prison I went to are filled with tinted, bullet and shatter-proof glass. They function as mirrors so you can know, understand every second you are there, you are watching yourself being watched. Still tinkering with Jeremy Bentham's *Panopticon*, the fathomless eye of his architectural fantasy holding everything captive and transforming captivity into a chamber of barely visible, cruel, and regulatory illuminations turned inward to make time seem more suspended, life floated away in a warehouse dementia of bodies encoded with penal routine to ensure a permanent uselessness anywhere other than this edge they've been left on. Except this prison was full of other kinds of hints, which came to disturb me, forced me to question all that I have come to know as an artist and the twentieth-century art that has moved me deeply and on which I have staked my life. This prison is immaculate. The floors are polished, burgundy-tinted concrete. The ceilings bear the marks of the molds that formed them and are painted white. The pipes that hang from those ceilings come in designer colors of lime-green, purple, and black. The combined glow of those pipes is tasteful, elegant, unobtrusively pure, and can be traced directly to the roots of modernism, and how, though it has been stated different ways, these ideas and images, which—although they may have at the moment of their original appearances, stood apart from the lure of advertising and product—are now at the core of mass distribution and wish formations that make need and commodity possible, especially this need, poised at the center of lifeless vengeance fantasies. The presence of "taste" here is employed in not only all of its commercial force as that force relates directly to prison, but its more hidden manifestations where such refinement rather than being the mistress of beauty becomes the mistress of arranged violation and obedience. The barred windows and their steel frames bespeak the most advanced architectural uses of materials and form. There is also a historical glow for me as a writer. At the beginning of my journey as an artist, I wanted to paint. In that desire I studied as much about the history of painting as I could. I still do. But I'm not a painter. In ways that I can't explain to this day, either to myself or anyone else, the explorations of those traditions I most revered turned me, to my own shock then because as a kid I had had such trouble with language and reading, toward writing. The architectural dimensions of this facility carry the echoes of twentieth-century art and what haunts it. For me, that shadow is one of absorptions. This art that has often been the source of much of my own personal transformation has also been reconceived as the primary imagery of an advertising and shopping culture. Up to the point before I entered these prisons, such a fact, though it often touched me with an angry though temporary doubt, held no permanence. But walking through this facility night after night made me realize how effectively the art of this century has been usurped. Prison now is as easily a part of our shopping impulses as the images of art, modernism, and postmodernism, and the condition of its most subtle parts became all too obvious through the design, construction, and generations-long realization of this maxi-max weighted with these artifacts. Bordering razor-wire and electrified fencing function rigorously as design, pattern, proportion. The razor-wire itself is part of an over-all esthetic consideration. It is a motif, decorative and sacrificial, ensnaring the eye and the would-be escapee. Those architects who brought it into being are sensitive, well trained, capable of designing a house with these materials, and creating a "look" that is as drastic, ironic, and seductive as the period in which we live.

"Bennie" was up for parole in two years. He used the remainder of the time inside to complete his Bachelor's degree. His work was strong, often original. The quality of the critique and analysis he applied to his thinking was disciplined, clear, had no unnecessary frills. He had absorbed the "requirements," stepped beyond them to train himself superbly, to ask questions, and to transpose those questions into a rigorous series of essays. Many of the men often asked for recommendations. The majority were for college, some for the parole board, others to the governor. No one I met in prison ever wanted to stay. The men who asked had worked toward their accomplishment. There was no reason not to write these recommendations based upon the experience I had had with them. I always emphasized that my letter was to be based on what I knew in the classroom and of the evolution of each student in the program. Those "letters" (mine and others) were often the foundation of further acceptance into graduate studies on the inside and outside. They might also contribute to a decision, on the part of the parole board, to release a prisoner.

One man I knew, for instance, had done eighteen hard years when he came into a course I taught on Herman Melville. He laughed over the prison he was now in, a maximum facility, that it was too loose, didn't deserve the name "prison." The diary he'd written was a drama of compassion and awakening, simple, direct, haunted by quiet truths:

> A prisoner is known to man as an object, not subject. In other words, the world is unaware of his inner circumstances, weaknesses, virtues, and finally presence. The things that lend meaning to his actions. All men, including felons, have inner depth others are not aware of . . . To be known merely as an object is to be unjustly known. One may feel incomplete, and do something irrational to fill the void . . . When a man is unknown he experiences solitude and a longing for death. For if you value yourself, but realize no one knows you, you might as well be dead. Thus, today's prisons breed desperate men.[33]

He got out, went to his family, shackled with a 24-hour, electronic-surveillance wristband. To my surprise, this man called me at my home one day, wanting nothing more than another letter, this time to a dean at a university near his hometown, for an honors program he was about to enter. It's been years, and I've heard nothing. Innumerable letters such as these were written; even though the program is "dead," I still on occasion get a request.

Bennie was different. His release was local. I didn't know that when I received his first call. He wanted a recommendation, too. The letter he wanted was to be addressed to a landlord. But this "landlord" was also different. She was an older, distinguished woman from a prominent black family. Before I'd even had a chance to compose the letter, I got a call from her. Her voice was filled with surety, dignity. The questions she was asking me had to do with Bennie and what kind of a young man I thought he was. I told her Bennie had been prisoner, that my experience with him was limited primarily to a classroom and to the essays he'd composed but that he'd been a fine student, responsible and mature, and that I hoped, based upon his real accomplishment, she'd offer him a chance to rent a room, do farm work on her land, enroll in a first semester of graduate studies. I told her, too, I did not know the nature of his crime. This elderly woman said Bennie had already done some work for her, done it well, and that she'd consider. I did not hear a word for weeks. When she called again, her voice was different. I asked quickly if anything had gone wrong, and she replied, "No. Not exactly," but did I know anything about his crime? I said once more, "No," as both her breath and mine dug a little more deeply. "Bennie was in prison for rape and sodomy," I heard her say. The moment I dreaded had come. My fears about a "Jack Abbott" and good intentions twisted and shriveled into hollow self-deception began to rise up and nearly choke me. These thoughts closed in on me many times during my years teaching in the program. They would appear and sink. But the vision of Norman Mailer, Jack Abbott, and the young aspiring actor who Abbott stabbed in the heart was never far away. For the second, as I heard the elderly woman breathing into her end of the phone, I thought my life might split open here. I didn't know if I'd be able to pick up what was left. "If I'd known that was his crime, I would have told you. There'd have been no question." She said, "I believe you," but whether or not the declaration was going to help I didn't know. "You haven't been attacked, have you?" The question was asked before I could grab it, keep it down. "No," she responded. "I don't want to hurt him or have him hurt, but I don't know what else to do. My lawyer believes I'm in danger and is bringing the police." I said I thought she was in danger, too. She felt terrible about the thing she wanted to do, to give this young black man a chance, that it would never be. I offered to come to her house immediately if she felt it was necessary. Bennie was evicted. He had committed no "crime" upon release, other than the one that had made him unacceptable to any community. Given what I know about habitual sex criminals, and knew then, too, nothing was worth such a chance. It was just dumb luck the irreversible had not taken place.

I have a sister-in-law who is a gifted psychologist. Her specialties cover not only the patients who see her but the pharmaceuticals they sometimes need. She worked with sex offenders for a number of years and her findings are not hopeful. Once the patterns of this disease set in, they become cumulative with each small, seemingly "harmless," act progressing toward more harmful behavior. The man whose obsessions focus on women and children, placed in a maximum-security prison, filled with men, will not act out. He can become a model prisoner, go to all the therapy required and demanded, and on paper look like a good candidate for parole. A parole board, in turn, does not always recognize how profoundly set this disease can be, how predatory and subtle. As a result, many of these men are granted release tragically to resume their predation once more. My sister-in-law, a tough professional, has stopped dealing with men whose patterns of illness she believes are often beyond cure.

After this incident, I called a woman I know—a specialist who works in and has organized prison-education programs—about Bennie. She is one of the most hardened prison experts I have come across, carefully aware of all personnel she must daily oversee, with a focus always upon the intrinsic humanity that was the program's primary calling. When I mentioned Bennie's name, there was a momentary silence. She took a controlling breath and said Bennie should have never been considered for parole, that he was a menace. The reporter Lawrence Wright, in an article entitled "A Rapist's Homecoming" in late 1995 in the *New Yorker* magazine, said, "Neither the criminal-justice system nor the mental-health system knows what to do with sex offenders, and neither wants to bear the responsibility for treating them."[34]

Chapter X
Keeplock

ONE BLOCK IN A PRISON where I was assigned a class had turned into a fuse. My assigned room was in that cell block, for "high-profile" inmates, the expert knife-maker, extortionist, escape artist, in-house pusher, general "incorrigible" ready to strike prisoners or guards (it made no difference). You could feel the desperation accumulating in the corners, on the window sills, spilling through the air ducts of the heating system. The facility was close to a riot.

One student in that block worked for years to get his Bachelor's and finally Master's degrees. "Wilfred" had been a community organizer in the inner city where he originally came from, a Black Panther. His picture eventually wound up on the FBI's Ten Most Wanted list. When he was finally captured, electrodes were applied to his body parts. His initial two years in prison were spent in a notorious Federal behavior-modification unit. He'd already done 14 years of a 25-to-life sentence when I met him, survived a number of riots, disastrous stretches in solitary confinement, and confrontations with prison guards that could easily have ended with his own murder. The intensity and desperation in that block were knots that wound steadily tighter by constant cell inspections, local facility directives whose minutia became an infection eating the spirit, and keeplock. It is said everyone in jail will do time in keeplock, or confinement in one's own cell. This form of torture even after a day reminds a man of the distance between himself and madness, surrounded as he is by the possessions he holds dear, the links with sanity receding among those last objects telling of another life. The senses shrink away, sight and hearing first, then touch, until these basic reassurances you're alive become shadow-smeared masks. It's the reason inmates lift weights, do push-ups, set-ups, finger dances, remind the mind to stay where it is. Some do it better; some just do it; some crank open the innocent little gate once.

Prison exists to destroy whoever enters. Under these conditions, critical mass can be no more than a refused small scoop of rice. Standard "feed-up procedure" was officially two scoops per man. You don't have to eat in prison, anyway. You can just "feed-up." The language mapping the ground you crawl on. One scoop of rice equals one pulled "red dot," the alarm grasped for riot or officer emergency or anything that means someone's going to get hurt. A lockdown began the day after the scoop incident, meaning all men in that block were confined to cells. Guards were assigned to bring food in Styrofoam trays and cups. Those cups and trays are the focus of convulsive pure hatred between the keepers and the kept, who feel the victuals are contaminated with shit, spit, or drops of urine waiting for a taste test. No one wants a riot in a New York State prison. Attica is a close, poisonous homeground no one forgets. Instead, this mess-hall incident ended in a nine-month strike based on four inmate demands. It could have turned at any moment into an unimaginable tragedy for guards and prisoners. During that period, the galleries of the block began to fill with garbage no one would clean up. For most of those months, civilians like myself were allowed inside, and the smell of filth penetrated everywhere. You'd see guards during class escorting inmates from the block three at a time—one officer, two guards for one shackled prisoner—while you'd be talking about Shakespeare, Ezra Pound's "Confucius," Tennessee Williams. Everything would go silent until those four bodies disappeared down a hall or past a window, their mutual annulment and exile so complete and purified the whole art of what it means to be alive loosened from its core.

Wilfred eventually transferred out of the Close Supervision Unit or CSU to another prison and an in-house Master's program. By this time, he'd spent over 20 years inside. His children had had children, his wife's accomplishments he attempted to share. But he knew. The missed voices, gestures, transitions moving his daughters and sons toward adulthood were unretrieved blanks. It was becoming an agony. All the prisoners I knew who had a family suffered. They wrote about it and talked about it.

A Master's student who had been in prison twenty-four years, commented in a study on "Imprisoned Fathers" about the numerous investigations and analyses of the "Black Family" in our culture, from Daniel Patrick Moynihan's *The Negro Family* to Lee Rainwater's *Behind Ghetto Walls*, which he felt at once describes this social body ". . . as a tangle of pathology . . . disorganized, functionally incompetent and negatively influencing its members attitudes, behaviors and values . . ." and requiring refutation. Yet the absent, demoralized black father in this picture of the "deviant" family was a sustained disfiguring termination for large numbers of these men, who in examining their own absences feared for their children and their wives. The essay I am quoting from and its

results are based on a study that was done in one of the maximum-
security prisons where I taught. Its basis was a questionnaire survey ".
. . administered to a randomly selected group of 327 inmates from a
total population of approximately 960 prisoners. The sample group
was drawn from an alphabetical roster of the total population for a
total of at least one third of the population . . ." Out of the 327 men,
263 chose to participate. Their response rate was over 80 percent. There
were refusals, transfers to other facilities, and detentions. Final participants were called in groups of forty to the "college" designated area, and
interviews were conducted on a one-to-one basis. Both questionnaire
and interviews demanded a painful honesty over their (whether black
or white) imprisoned fathers' relationships with their children. For
those fathers, in spite of what were often the strongest efforts possible,
the findings presented detailed accounts of relationships receding into
frustrated, increasingly more unreachable distances. But these results,
the author says, ". . . will have important implications for social services, psychologists, sociologists and prison administration policy mak-
ers who are concerned with . . . humane institutional practices, and
concrete programs for imprisoned fathers and their families."[35]

The details of these and many other examinations conducted by
present and former prisoners demonstrate the unusual importance of
the programs for higher education in our prisons for the designers of
social policy and the public. These findings, along with prison-education programs themselves, have been "killed," and we can pretend
that neither really matters. On the basis of that pretension, however,
we can ask, in this atmosphere of retributions, what are the borders
of punishment? Do the definitions of those borders stop at the mind
and body of the convicted person, or do they spread beyond to include

his or her family, whose members are innocent, and become themselves victims through the total body of negligence our retributions create? Do we want a democracy whose mission will be nothing more than a sum of legal fictions rooted in the ideology of reprisals and what those reprisals will come to dignify? Wilfred and his co-defendant, "Stephen," committed a notorious crime, one that went to the central joint of racial hatred and frustration that detonated in the 1960s and early 1970s. Stephen became a Sufi mystic, studying the works of the great medieval Muslim philosophers and poets, and came to a moment in his cell where most of his mind fell into the abyss. The leftover fragment had to pull the rest out, and from what I understood that took years. Wilfred received his Master's degree and keeps examining the law in search of a hearing that might re-open his and Stephen's case, a freedom, which in reality, may never be granted.

Chapter XI
Gail

THE TOWN WHERE I LIVE on the western edge of the Catskills has a Lenni Lenape name that means "Land of Running Waters." Rivers, rivulets, and streams cut everywhere through these ancient hills. Brook trout in mid-summer search out the deepest, coolest pools and flinch away before even the slightest edging shadows. They know the rocks, grass overhangs, and whirlpools in the creek bordering our land. So do the ugly-tempered, brown, fast as lightning water snakes that hunt them and reach a length of five feet. The tide marks of earlier deluges are also scourings from the glacial melt forming the wash of the present interglacial canyon lying upslope and beyond a meadow filled in autumn with wild turkey.

The Esopus Creek that runs down slope from the mountain we live on is one of the finest trout streams on the continent. Further west lies the east branch of the Delaware River. In the hidden valleys it courses through, there are small lakes and often, if you look close, you'll find the stones the ancient Indians used for net weights. Coming home from prison at about 30 miles per hour, I hit a bear once near the Esopus Creek, or maybe it hit me. My car and I were in the way of the newly sprouted rhubarb it wanted to get to. I saw it out the

corner of my left eye, thought at first it was the biggest dog ever. It
slammed into the steel and glass around the front light, then peed all
over what remained, itself, and nearly me, then ran, no limp, and no—
what I was most afraid of—broken back. The thought of a wounded
bear scared me. I'd grown up with bear stories. The legends of the California Grizzly, those animals' ferocity, intelligence, and power still
weave through my childhood and manhood. I found a local cop, and
we searched the weeds and shallow gullies, discovering nothing. He
asked if the bear could run after impact, and I said it had. "It'll go for
water then; lie in a running stream belly down to heal whatever injuries
it might've got."

Nearly all the waters where my family lives run straight east to the
Hudson River and its estuaries. The Esopus is one of the primary feeder
streams, and its liquids, rather than joining the great river directly as
they did for thousands of years, now supply the main fill for the
Ashokan Reservoir. This marvel of engineering drowned a number of
towns at the beginning of the twentieth century. Local chronicles tell
about New York City officials who set homes to torch with everything
still in them but their owners and how a local rash of suicides appeared
as the damned streams slowly engulfed the Ashokan Valley, its forest
and farms, the life that it once held to be replaced as a supply of fresh
water for the City of New York. I've lived in and visited a number of
American cities. The best drinking water is New York's. I didn't understand why until I saw reservoirs such as the Pepacton, the Montgap,
and the Ashokan. Each of these bodies of water is a huge lake. The
land and mountainscapes that surround them have a particular, inti-
mate beauty filled with the subtleties of rarely seen scarlet tanagers
perched on a creek-edged boulder, an otter stilled in midstream of a

high wash by the branch you've just snapped with a too-heavy step, a wild turkey amazed over a first-seen human. My route to prison took me over the Ashokan, so I'd see it swell and shrink with drought and flood. Fishermen in their motorless boats poised, hardly discernible in the far solitude where they'd thrown a light anchor, and near, closer to shore, a bass up from the depths caught in the sun, six to eight feet long. The overlooking mountain forests equally swell with their life and sleep. New leafage in spring brings with it flower scented airs, wild perfumes differently introduced week by week until at least late August when the great autumn change begins, winds going drier and cooler, the waters of our swimming hole tinged with hints of ice not yet appeared, but unstoppable, on the way.

Catskills in full leaf have a gentle engreened surface. They can almost fool you. Below the canopy slopes are hard, strewn with banks of small cliff every 25 or 30 yards, steep. Look closer, and there's hardly any food, and what there is comes stingy and hidden. On one mountain adjacent to ours, there is a species of rattlesnake, stuck on this micro-island from another age. These serpents can get to be ten feet long and slide through the berry bushes rooted to top-most shale slabs. But they're not interested in the berries. It's birds. Food preference and evolution have provided them with extraordinarily potent toxins for air-borne feasts that might otherwise, even though they'll die, end up too far away, in the last panic flight, to be traced down. Get a main vein puncture from one of these reptiles, and you can start counting the seconds of your time. From hibernation to hibernation, the hunt's too compressed, though, for wasteful inter-species encounters, so they're shy, rare, don't want any trouble. Up on the top slopes, who stays alive and who doesn't has another exacting face. Wild turkey and deer share the same environment and sometimes food. Acorns are the object. The prize—who gets to breathe at the end of the last, desperate two or three weeks of winter before the robins come in a sporadic singleness, when there's nothing. The turkey is the smartest game bird. It knows where you are, can run or fly, has experienced, jittery scouts and will out-compete the habit-bound, less intelligent deer. My favorite time of year is when the leaves have fallen along with their sap, the world gone to root, sleep, and partial rot for the spring to come. I can see the fully exposed ridges then that encircle the upper meadows where I live. Bear have dug themselves in, under tree or ledge, and you'll catch the bristle edge of a coyote behind a now leafless maple or blending into a soiled, rock-fissured crest. Deer have gone from tawny brown to gray, and they can emerge out of morning fog and mist as if they were ancestral shadows come with irresistible invitation, ears flitting, twisting for any sound that'll tell them to run. The forest and grasses in the lower meadows when the birch leaves begin to yellow from killing frosts smell like figs that've gone unpicked and dropped, their over-ripe weight severing them from the mothering tree. A fern going from its ancient green to burnt brown means to me these hard mountains will become more like a desert. I can see boulders, faraway cliffs; the stripped trees and their barrenness are a familiar beauty and a reminder of beauty's strange and mysterious prices.

My walks in Indian summer often take me to the ruins of a farm abandoned in the 1840s. The apple trees those settlers planted are now remnants twisted into raw, tight facts, the flesh of their trunks half-gouged by time and woodpeckers and spiders, their standing itself a bewilderment. Bite into the fruit, and you'll at once get a sweet-tart taste clinging to and cleansing your palate. There's nothing like it on the commercial market. It's small, insect-resistant, pale green, disshaped. At the end of a long hike, those apples are quiet, open gifts. They are a last evidence of preoccupation and limit that could find no anchor here, stone returned to itself everywhere else again except in the shy, barely notched statement of fulfillment locked in these apples.

During the years of my experience in the prisons I realized that the ice-scoured, ancient landscape I have lived in and grown deeply to love has become an experiment not dissimilar to my native Mohave desert where large tracts of that space have been given over to the reserve of bomb and strafing run, "no man's lands" pocked with these wasting residues. The forests and valleys of New York are slowly being transformed into penal strips with dependent local populations having at last nowhere else to go for employment, future, or choice. They're like the abandoned farm I've walked over so many times, a last evidence, too, of preoccupation, loss of anchorage, and drastic limit for the populations going into surplus and the designs of "use" which await them.

On awards days at the end of each school year, you'd see grandmothers, fathers, sisters, nieces, children. The food for those occasions came out of the prisoners' own pockets. The kids were beautifully dressed, adults proud, the grief over absence softened, guards everywhere with walkie-talkies and batons. I asked my wife, Gail, if she'd want to go to a prison, to one of those awards days when the men received their degrees. She wasn't sure. The distance between the actual faces and faceless names she'd heard for years was one she preferred. She thought about it for a week, asked nervous questions, and said, "Yes." With that, I got proper clearance, and on Saturday morning in a mid-May we set out over the Ashokan, through Kripplebush, down into Kerhonkson, and over Minnewaska. It was the route I had taken for years to get to Shawangunk. When Gail saw the prison, she went silent, but as we got closer the sight of children, grandmothers, families made the passage seem easier.

The routine upon entering is that all inessential personal belongings are put in lockers. Bodies, clothes, purses are examined by metal detectors. Names are verified. Shoes are taken off and turned upside-down. The abrupt, short-tempered voices of angry guards made the single-room entry building go instantly sour and snarled. An officer that day seemed particularly enraged. His color was white, and he was concentrating on a young black woman coming to visit a husband, a brother, an uncle—no one knew. He was making her re-do paper work, repeatedly asking questions, moving toward overt verbal abuse. The young woman, realizing what was taking place, backed away, looked the officer in the face, and said, "Mister, you're beginning to scare me." The silence in the room, the stares of the visitors, stopped the guard. He had done his work, and though this kind of abuse of visitors and especially family members of incarcerated prisoners is illegal, it is still permitted. The practice is designed to humiliate and spread punishment to those who are innocent, to equate close relationship with guilt and the patterns of contempt guilt presumably deserves.

There is a necessity for security in a prison, for a detailed search of all incoming persons, clothes, shoes, bags. Drugs as well as weapons can be easily smuggled in and become a danger for guards and convicts; people have died because of these failures of procedure. In the nearly ten years of my work in the prisons, there was not one entrance in which such detailed scrutiny was overlooked. It took time. Bags had to be emptied, coats examined, books opened and gone through, belts and shoes taken off, wallets opened. This normal prison greeting was always done with courtesy, and, with the guards I also came to know, with humor. The abuse I am describing, and which my wife unfortunately witnessed, is not uncommon. The officer was reprimanded and sent to another section of the prison. Great damage is created. The prisoners hear about these incidents, get the names of the corrections officers, and hatred on both sides twists and can become, in the instance of a white officer's ugly address to a young black woman, an inescapable progression leading to injury and death. It is a job smothered in stress. Often the officers are young men from rural backgrounds, poorly trained to deal psychologically with the urban black and Latino prisoners. Their rural assumptions and racial attitudes are a barely hidden undersurface that in itself poses a threat to security.

"Abdul," who completed his Bachelor's degree in spite of a life sentence, worked as an orderly in a prison office. The secretaries were cold, constantly surly, and for months never let up until he, a black man, turned on them, one day, and asked what he had done to them. There was no real "answer." In response, he actually took the time to explain that what he had done had ended at least 25 years before and that two lives were destroyed, his and another man's. "I've been courteous, done what you've asked, and kept silent," he told the secretaries, "and yet you somehow take personally something I did over 25 years in the past, that has nothing to do with you. Why?"

The answer to that "why?" may be found in the media's normalization of a specialized hysteria in which the violent acts of separate and now monstrous populations that are, in turn, the media's fabrication, become "personal." The weight of that "personal" totality is anchored to our dinner tables, our feelings of domestic longing, the safety of our hearths. The racial make-up of this specialized hysteria is almost impossible to avoid. The media's fabrication has created a "proximity" where there is less and less room for any of us as citizens to maneuver or think. The "proximity" is a punishment in itself that breeds other punishments, other retributions for a society whose thirsts for retribution are inviting a blueprint and mystification for "values" that may become a background for a new set of initial wrongs a twenty-first or twenty-second century may also have to struggle through. We have already had 500 years to devise one set of wrongs. A new order of ensnarements can just as easily permeate and undermine the centuries not yet arrived, as it already has the centuries we have supposedly left behind. The abusive prison guard should have been fired. He wasn't. His contribution of more poison to poison is acceptable.

That awards day, a representative from the prison came to escort me and Gail. We spent three hours listening to invocations, speeches, and awards ceremonies. Those rituals were punctuated with a lunch for the prisoners' families, guests, ministers, rabbis, and special visitors, such as my wife. Men whom I had described to her for years came up, introduced themselves, their wives and children, and spent time to talk. One of the best blues singers I've ever heard performed that day, a man who learned in the program how to read and write, who got his Bachelor's degree, and who, as far as I know, is out. Gail met poets, playwrights, musicians, struggling students, heard stories, spoke to wives and grandmothers, and when we walked out of that prison to re-traverse our route through the mountains home, she could barely talk.

No one can predict how someone else will feel after this kind of experience. Many of the prisoners she met had been violent and dangerous. A man who sat next to her committed a particularly grisly murder when he was young. Many others were condemned for non-violent drug offenses. Gail is still, after years, dealing with a day that will not grant easy legitimacy to any of the emotions she felt, including her revulsion over the wasted lives. I'm not often sure whether or not I should have asked her to go with me that morning, but I wanted her to know where I went and what it meant, if that can ever be known.

Chapter XII
Massai

AT THE UNIVERSITY of Oklahoma, there is an Archive of Western History. It is one of the finest collections of its kind in the world. A small, obscure book is housed there. Its paper and glues have gone brittle since its publication in 1887. But this book holds a story about the life history of the nation, and although much of this story remains unwanted still, its constrained murmur continues to unfold. The author's name was Herbert Welsh, and he titled the writing *The Apache Prisoners in Fort Marion, St. Augustine, Florida*. Fort Marion was the end of another train ride in the nineteenth century. It was called Fort San Marco prior to its use as a concentration camp for various Indian peoples. This old-time fortress with moat, bastions, and watch-towers was built not from stone but coquina, a composition of sand and tiny shells. The bewildered men, women, and children who would be held behind its walls were forced into trains that carried them thousands of miles from the remote plains and deserts of their origins. Many of them had never seen such a machine. They were terrified by soldiers eager to kill them, by the thought of mass executions at the end of a journey they could never have imagined, and by being shut in closed, jammed railroad cars without air or water as they rolled through the deserts of the southwest and the swamps of the deep south. A white guard watching over the Chiricahua Apache commented that nobody but an Indian could have put up with the stench. The outbreak of tuberculosis that would kill most of these people in their Fort Marion captivity may have begun on that train. None of these people could have known either about the language that had come to engulf them. Herbert Welsh said the purpose of his documentation was to represent ". . . methods for the solution of the Indian problem. . . ." The America of the nineteenth century in its genocidal episode had invented the language of the twentieth. The only adjective missing here is "final."

There was no need for that. The "finality" that had taken place before the train journeys was so complete it needed no reference, breath to sound it, or syntax to place it. The location of the adjective and its apocalypse wander continuously over a geography we will not to this day trace or name. It is the one defining difference between ourselves and the Nazis, who in offering the adjective its placement submitted their nation, in spite of their intentions, to grief and admission of guilt. This omission from our vocabulary and utterance always has made a "solution" easy. In letting the noun "loosen" us from our civil and communal rootages, it may no longer become possible for a telling adjective to find anchorage before it, and we can, with the upholstery a "New Jack" language offers, begin even more appropriately to "customize" our solutions and our target surplus populations.

Fort Marion is a larger story because it was the site of *END* for so many others, including the Kiowa, Cheyenne, and Arapaho, who were shipped there in 1875 and left a chronicle of their disappeared world through a series of magnificent drawings they were allowed to produce, now called the *Plains Indian Art from Fort Marion*. Some of their names were *Bear's Heart, Koba, Shingled Hair, Zotom* or "Biter," *Squint Eyes, Wohaw,* which in Kiowa is "Beef"; *Cohoe,* "Lame" in Cheyenne, *Big Nose, Shave Head,* and *Good Talk*.[36] In 1886, an Apache named Massai decided to escape from a train carrying him and others toward St. Louis and the Mississippi. He pried the windows loose and jumped out into the rolling hill country of eastern Missouri. He traced his way home at least 1,500 miles over land and rivers he'd never seen. In all those towns and densely farmed spaces, nobody saw this lone Apache escapee, who found what food he could. His fellow tribesmen described his skills as being only "average." Perhaps the Apache were hinting at something else. Had Massai been endowed with a finer skill and as ugly a sense of retribution as his former captors, he could have caused real harm. A lone, gifted warrior was a master of silence and death, capable of running at least 70 miles a day with little food or water, and leaving no hint of his passage. But without family, tribe, or land, there would have been no reason to choose such wasteful violence. In that, the inhabitants were lucky Massai made it back to the remote and beloved terrain of the southwest where he hid out for years as an outrider until he was eventually killed.

Fort Marion, with its yellow fever, tuberculosis, stifling heat, and swamps, was an ideal banishment for the unfortunate others who were incapable of any kind of escape, primarily because their whole families were with them, so such abandonment would have been unthinkable. Included among those 500 men, women, and children were the Chiricahua scouts who, with a promise of amnesty, had faithfully assisted the United States troops. Ki-e-ta and Martinez, rotting among all the rest, were the two to whom Geronimo had personally surrendered.

In June of 1995, I went to the last graduation and awards ceremony for the prison education program at Wallkill. There will be no more programs of this kind. Their proof and the possibilities for change and renewal they offered have been seen finally as a threat and waste. The monies for books and tuition were "killed" by the 1994 Clinton crime bill. A man I've known for a long time was there. He'd been transferred from a maximum to this medium and was on his way out after 18 years. He, too, had begun learning to read and to write in a composition course. He was fighting for his life those many years ago like all the rest of the men I knew. His fight also included one against cancer. The diagnosis clarified what kind, and chemotherapy was being administered. His cancer, fortunately, seems to be gone. He has his Bachelor's degree and will get out to pursue the rest of his higher education. The example he set inspired others and gave them the nerve to begin to overcome the profound debilitation prison imposes.

The men fortunate enough to get their degrees that day were in grief over the death of these programs. Their peers, who wanted to follow them, now may never have the chance. Prison education was a necessary lifeline for these prisoners, their families, and the worlds they came from. It also brought a stability and atmosphere of respect. Prisons will become more dangerous. The small refusals and strikes that leak into the news may lead to another Attica, the largest single episode of Americans killing Americans since the Civil War. A repetition of an Attica-like riot or riots will mark the beginning of an exile, withdrawal, and collapse of promise to bring to fruition the map of civil well-being that belongs to all of us. If we are going to abandon a part of our population and make of them a surplus body fated in their generations to be shipped to prison colonies, then we must consider how much of this abandonment at the core of our traditions involves ourselves, at the deepest levels of privacy and dream. Asked in a recent speech about the inherent violence in our earliest ancestors, Richard Leakey responded with the only evidence he has seen. The paleontologist referred to fossil hominid femurs that had once been broken and then, in their healing, fused over a million years ago. The only way those bones could have healed over was through someone taking care of someone else over the long months of recuperation. The search for an inherent or genetic predisposition for violence to explain the crisis of our civilization disintegrates before these fragile and accidentally composed remains. If there is any predisposition we seem truly to have inherited, Mr. Leakey stated, "It is for compassion." I want to be reassured by such a statement. The pictures of those femurs come close to me and help the damage of events to recede. But such a reassurance is finally not true, not enough though the regrowth of that bone, far away as it is, sounds a story of recovery locked in the realm of the unlistenable.

Our civil well-being is being destroyed by something strange and distant and sickening. Its failure for every culture that uses it is its triumph steeped in the worship of safe conduct and the violations that inevitably are the sum of such wishes, and where our practices of convenience and guarantee begin to assume, through themselves, a new presence of force we have, until now, been able to contain. All the bodies it has ever and will ever hold help it to become, in this moment of our abandonment, most beautiful when it is most dead. We have no way to gauge its scale or its damage, and its despotism, to call up de

Tocqueville's words, assumes a different character in our days, more extensive and more mild. Because of that, its degradations are absolute and reside in us absolutely without torment.

Shandaken, New York
April 12, 1997

Afterword

SINCE 1997 when the first edition of this book was published, the prison industry has continued to grow. We have seen its menace spread to Iraq and have still failed to comprehend that these terrible photographs are the images of our failure as a People who have allowed this major domestic industry to injure and reduce our Democracy beyond recognition. Perhaps the division of our nation we see taking place in this time is based on the possibility that one population's urgent need for Democracy either can be conveniently ignored or partially forgotten and that another part of our population needs the Democracy more now than at any other time in our history. The Democracy has utterly failed to include this segment of our People. This loss and waste, as I have tried to say in this book, has no boundary; and such erasure makes hatred, brutality, fear, and disenfranchisement into unquestioned convenience. The Abu Ghraib crisis is ours, no matter how much we might choose to ignore it, and no matter how sneakily politicians on both sides of the aisle might choose to hide it.

The investment in punishment has created an Industry of Punishment we are now dependent upon, which strains our resources and capacities to imagine another kind of economics and to even imagine we once had a humanity.

Is it this drastic?

The answer is to attempt to truthfully appraise the few pictures from Abu Ghraib we have been allowed to see and to try to recognize this is not an aberration; to realize that these are the common practices of a world we have created and choose not to see, or believe cannot exist.

Can we begin to restore rehabilitation programs that include both extensive educational and vocational training, which reverse the emphasis on punishment and security? Can we reverse the detention practices in the juvenile facilities, where children are isolated in their cells for more than 200 days a year and where juvenile wards receive almost none of the required teaching and counseling which could keep them from returning to prison; where beatings are commonplace?

The answer is "yes," but only a qualified "yes." We must now deal with the propaganda and games of ignorance that have brought us all to this bewildering and dangerous crossroads in the life of our nation.

Because the costs have become so burdensome, we are beginning to question the penal system's senseless descent into betrayal and stupidity. The state of Missouri has created new, sensitive approaches toward juvenile offenders that show much promise for rehabilitation and drastic reduction of recidivism rates. Many states, including California, with the incomprehensible disaster of its juvenile detention policies, are researching the results and policies in Missouri. This does represent some hope for reversal and change. At the same time there are calls for prison reform in California, which has the largest and most costly prison industry in the world, to increase the amount of job-training, education, and counseling. California's prisoners suffer a 60 percent recidivism rate, the highest in a nation that imprisons 1/4 of the world's prisoners. There are as yet no details for how these proposed programs might be implemented and managed, nor how the vast number of employees in the prison system will be re-trained for new jobs.

We have enchained ourselves to a labyrinth. The questions involved in our abilities as citizens to recognize what we have done to our daily lives and to our nation remain unanswered and hidden.

San Diego, California

January 10, 2005

Notes

[1]Václav Havel, *Living in Truth*, ed. Jan Vladislav (New York: Faber and Faber, 1986).

[2]Paulette Thomas, "Making Crime Pay: Triangle of Interests Creates Infrastructure to Fight Lawlessness." *The Wall Street Journal*, 12 May 1994.

[3]David Nickell, "Wackenhut Pushes for Prison Jobs." *South Florida Business Journal Inc.*, 2 May 1988 question as to "880502."

[4]Marc Mauer, *Americans Behind Bars: The International Use of Incarceration, 1992-1993* (Washington, D.C.: The Sentencing Project, 1994).

[5]Ibid.

[6]Thomas Jefferson, letter to Col. William S. Smith, 13 November 1787. *The Papers of Thomas Jefferson*, Vol. 12, ed. Julian P. Boyd (Princeton, New Jersey: Princeton University Press, 1955).

[7]William Blake, *The Poetry and Prose of William Blake*, ed. David V. Erdmann (New York: Doubleday, 1965).

[8]Mauer.

[9]Blake.

[10]*Tocqueville and Beaumont on Social Reform*, comp. Seymour Drescher (New York: Harper & Row, 1968). See also Gustave de Beaumont and Alexis de Tocqueville, *On the Penitentiary System in the United States and Its Application in France* (New York: Augustus M. Kelley Publishers, 1970).

[11]Ibid.

[12]Nils Christie, *Crime Control as Industry* (London: Routledge, 1994).

[13]Robert Duncan, *Ground Work, Before the War* (New York: New Directions, 1984).

[14]Materials based on prisoner's essay. See also William H. Hallahan, *Misfire: The History of How America's Small Arms Have Failed Our Military* (New York: Scribner's, 1994).

[15]Robert S. McNamara with Brian VanDeMark, *In Retrospect: The Tragedy and Lessons of Vietnam* (New York: Vintage, 1995).

[16]Promotional letter sent to author, The American Correctional Association, 1997. Exhibitor information. American Correctional Association, Lanham, Maryland, March, 1997.

[17]Material based on prisoner's essay.

[18]Lee Rainwater and William Yancey, eds., *The Moynihan Report and the Politics of Controversy* (Cambridge, Massachusetts: MIT Press, 1967).

[19]Alexis de Tocqueville, *Democracy in America*, Vols. I and II (New York: Random House, 1990).

[20]Ibid.

[21]John M. Vanyur, "Design Meets Mission at New Federal Max Facility," *Corrections Today*, July, 1995.

[22]Charles Dickens, *American Notes for General Circulation* (New York: Viking Penguin, 1974).

[23]Christie.

[24]Ibid.

[25]Ibid.

[26]Ibid.

[27]The comments by Falwell and Helms made in the late 1980s appeared as part of a series of window installations in 1987 at The New Museum of Contemporary Art in New York City. These installations included *SILENCE=DEATH* symbols invented by the AIDS activist groups "Gran Fury" and "ACT-UP." These powerful symbols and other media forms were used to build awareness of the AIDS holocaust.

[28]Michel Foucault, *Discipline & Punish: The Birth of the Prison* (New York: Vintage, 1995).

[29]Ibid.

[30]Ibid.

[31]Reinaldo Arenas, *Before Night Falls: A Memoir* (New York: Penguin, 1994).

[32]Material based on prisoner's essay.

[33]Material based on prisoner's essay.

[34]Lawrence Wright, "A Rapist's Homecoming," *The New Yorker* 4 September 1995.

[35]Material based on prisoner's essay for a Master's degree.

[36]Karen Daniels Petersen, *Plains Indian Art, from Fort Marion* (Norman, Oklahoma: University of Oklahoma Press, 1971). See also Angie Debo, *Geronimo* (Norman: University of Oklahoma Press, 1976).

Introduction Source Notes

"Where California's Prisons Flourish," Peter Schrag, (Editorial, *Sacramento Bee*, July 2004)

"Prisons No Place for the Mentally Ill," Jamie Fellner and Sasha Abramsky (Editorial, *San Diego Tribune*, February 13, 2004)

"Justice System Broken," Henry Weinstein (*Los Angeles Times*, June 24, 2004)

Bureau of Justice Statistics

"Jail Rate for Young Black Men Sets Mark," Fox Butterfield (New York Times News Service, July, 2004)

"Panel Urges Revamp of State Prisons," Jennifer Warren and Tim Reiterman (*Los Angeles Times*, July 2004)

"Prison Guards are Accused of Code of Silence," Dan Thomas (Associated Press, *San Diego Tribune*, March 29, 2004)

"More Inmates Serving Life Terms," (Associated Press, *San Diego Tribune*, May 12, 2004)

"Prison Abuses," Editorial (*San Diego Tribune*, February 2004)

"Dismal California Prisons Hold Juvenile Offenders," John M. Broder (*New York Times*, Sunday February 15, 2004)

"Prison Problems," Editorial (*San Diego Tribune*, January 27, 2004)

"Deal Gives Guards Millions in Benefits," Dan Morain (*Los Angeles Times*, July 13, 2004)

"Study Finds More Mentally Ill are in Jail than in Hospitals," Fox Butterfield (New York Times News Service, October 22, 2003)

About the Author

NOVELIST, POET, AND ESSAYIST DAVID MATLIN has taught literature and creative writing at San Diego State University since 1997. His books of poetry include *Fontana's Mirror, Dressed In Protective Fashion,* and *China Beach.* His first novel, *How the Night is Divided,* was nominated for a National Book Critics Circle Award. This book on prisons in America is based on the author's seventeen-year residence in the Hudson Valley and Catskill Mountains of New York State.